# RESPECTING THE PUPIL

## ESSAYS ON TEACHING ABLE STUDENTS

# ⌐Respecting the Pupil⌐

## ESSAYS ON TEACHING
## ABLE STUDENTS

BY MEMBERS OF THE FACULTY
OF PHILLIPS EXETER ACADEMY

Donald B. Cole and Robert H. Cornell, Editors

The Phillips Exeter Academy Press

RESPECTING THE PUPIL: ESSAYS ON TEACHING ABLE
STUDENTS. Copyright © 1981 by the Trustees of Phillips Exeter
Academy. All rights reserved. Printed in the United States of
America. No part of this book may be used or reproduced in any
manner whatsoever without written permission except in the
case of brief quotations embodied in critical notes and reviews.
For information address The Phillips Exeter Academy Press,
Publisher, c/o The Director of Publications, Phillips Exeter
Academy, Exeter, N.H. 03833.

Library of Congress Cataloging in Publication Data

Respecting the pupil.

    Includes bibliographical references

    1. Phillips Exeter Academy.   2. Talented students —
New Hampshire.  I. Cole, Donald B.  II. Cornell, Robert H.
III. Phillips Exeter Academy.

LD7501.E936R47         371.95         ' 81-81104
ISBN O-939618-01-X                         AACR2

81 82 83 84 10 9 8 7 6 5 4 3 2 1

# TABLE OF CONTENTS

*[Continued]*

*I believe that our own experience instructs us that the secret of Education lies in respecting the pupil. It is not for you to choose what he shall know, what he shall do. It is chosen and foreordained, and he only holds the key to his own secret. By your tampering and thwarting and too much governing he may be hindered from his end and kept out of his own. Respect the child. Wait and see the new product of Nature. Nature loves analogies, but not repetitions. Respect the child. Be not too much his parent. Trespass not on his solitude.*

*But I hear the outcry which replies to this suggestion: — Would you verily throw up the reins of public and private discipline; would you leave the young child to the mad career of his own passions and whimsies, and call this anarchy a respect for the child's nature? I answer, — Respect the child, respect him to the end, but also respect yourself. Be the companion of his thought, the friend of his friendship, the lover of his virtue, — but no kinsman of his sin. Let him find you so true to yourself that you are the irreconcilable hater of his vice and the imperturbable slighter of his trifling.*

Ralph Waldo Emerson
in "Education,"
*The Works of
Ralph Waldo Emerson*
1883

# INTRODUCTION

Donald B. Cole and Robert H. Cornell

EMERSON HAS ALWAYS HAD the knack of speaking anew to each generation of Americans. When he writes that "the secret of Education lies in respecting the pupil," he speaks as much for teaching today as for teaching in the 19th century. His admonition is particularly appropriate for those engaged in teaching talented, able students, for success in educating them lies more in helping them find ways to develop their talents themselves than it does in molding them rigidly. The emphasis should be on learning rather than on teaching. The teachers at Phillips Exeter Academy who wrote these essays on teaching able students focus their attention on respecting the pupil.

Emerson, however, was realistic enough to know that his admonition might be misinterpreted. He answered those who would accuse him of neglecting what he called "discipline," what we call "content," by adding the second paragraph outlining his belief in the role of the teacher and the importance of subject matter. "Respect the child," he told the teachers, "but also respect yourself." Our authors also balance their concern for the student with a vigorous defense of the teacher and of academic content. They do not believe, to quote one writer, in "working in a vacuum." Instead they believe that educating the talented is a cooperative enterprise in learning in which the students and the teacher work together and respect one another.

Since this book is concerned with teaching the talented, it should begin with a definition of the word "talented" — a difficult task because the meaning has been obscured by popular stereotype, because talent exists in so many forms and because the definition must be subtle, tentative and based as much on intuition as on objective data. But it is a task worth attempting because students with talent have so much to offer.

We are not, first of all, limiting our definition to geniuses — those special people born with a natural gift possessed by only a few — Mozart, Einstein, Shakespeare. The popular stereotype of the gifted genius is not much help in a book on teaching the talented because there are not enough of these geniuses to make such a limited study worthwhile. We are not, on the other hand, eliminating such persons from our consideration — geniuses also need to learn.

Talent, furthermore, exists in many forms, and few students are truly talented in more than one area. Students with mathematical talent are ordinarily separate from those with verbal talent; both are distinct from those with linguistic talent; and, as David Coffin points out, the linguistically talented come in two forms. Artistic talent is a special case, for, in the words of Jacques Barzun, art is "a mode of thought without words, inarticulate, *sui generis.*"[1] So also is athletic talent, which differs from the others. Even in a school with many able students, most of the students in a given class will lack a high degree of talent in that particular subject.

Within these discrete forms talent is difficult to define because it is so special, so personal. The talented athlete is not simply fast, or strong, or possessed of eye and muscle coordination. There is also something special, something instinctive, something unmeasurable about a talented athlete. In a similar way the talented musician has more than physical coordination; there is more to musical talent than simply performing a piece correctly; the talented musician puts a personal stamp of artistry on the piece.

The same sort of personal intuitive qualities are also present in those with intellectual talent. Those whom we call talented verbally, linguistically, or mathematically make inferences, analogies, and relationships better than their classmates. They qualify more, they make distinctions, they see the gray areas where others see only the distinct hues. They make better hypotheses or informed guesses; they synthesize more often. They are often quicker than the other students, often more impatient; they do not want to be taught what they already know. They love information, content, and enjoy collecting data.

---

1. Jacques Barzun, "Art and Educational Inflation," *Occasional Paper 25* (Washington, D.C., Council for Basic Education, 1979), p. 9.

Those with talent are, above all, more curious, more observant, and often more alert than their classmates. Talent is such a subtle matter that teachers should hesitate before deciding who is or is not talented.

The essays that follow deal with teaching students who have a degree of talent in a specific area. They are students with an unusual capacity to accomplish something; they have aptitude in some area. They have artistic or physical skills or they are talented verbally or linguistically or mathematically. Above all they are highly motivated. The essays have a broad application, for many of the modes of teaching are effective also for the less than talented. Not all the students at Phillips Exeter or any school are truly talented even in one area. We are writing about able, hard-working young men and women.

In describing how to teach these able students our authors show remarkable agreement. Even though the writers were selected to represent their disciplines, their essays are not parochial. The emphases were so similar that we decided to arrange the essays thematically instead of by subject matter. In Part I we have combined essays that stress the importance of the students in educating the talented. Part II, however, makes it clear that the teachers believe in content, in subject matter. The two essays linked in Part III describe the use of inductive strategies and call for teaching the process of investigation. Those in Part IV describe teaching techniques in detail and emphasize the necessity of allowing talented students to move rapidly. And in the final section, we have presented three essays that focus on educating the whole student, not just training the mind or the body. The arrangement of essays is more suggestive than definitive. Any one of the essays could have logically been included in several other parts — some in all. But we believe that our arrangement and our topical quotations accurately suggest the central arguments of the book.

Most important of all is belief in student participation — both individually and as a group. Nowhere is the emphasis more evident than in Norval Rindfleisch's essay on teaching English, in which he stresses the importance, even the indispensability, of student writing. Rindfleisch wants students to write because he considers writing the most active of all intellectual tasks and because he believes that students learn best if they are active. Students must not only write by themselves, but they must then share their writing with their classmates. In a similar vein Mary DeVault and David McIlhiney argue that religion is best taught if students in small groups grapple with the meaning of religious texts. Donald Schultz makes the same argument for teaching drama, where student participation is the very basis of the pedagogy.

In this student-centered scheme of education the teacher must not dominate the class, must not rely upon authority, fear, or didactic forms of teaching. Janet Kehl declares bluntly that the student, not the teacher, must play the most active role in class; and Rindfleisch urges his colleagues to let the students talk and not to be afraid of moments of silence. Irving Forbes even admits that on some occasions he tells musicians that he has no comment to make about their performances; instead he asks the other members of the class to provide the critique.

The essayists, however, do not ask teachers to be ciphers or to abandon responsibility for what goes on in class. They want the teacher to play an important role, but they want it to be the role of a Socrates rather than that of a lecturer in a medieval university. The teacher is there to help talented students learn as part of the class — not to tell them exactly what they should learn. The essayists encourage the teacher to dare, to risk the absence of form, to do with less structure and less dogma. For them the teacher is a partner in learning, a subtle combination of questioner, inspiration, scholar, and colleague.

Nor do the essays recommend teaching without content, for they show a deep respect for solid academic material. As Arthur Gilcreast writes, "it is the content that offers the setting" for helping students develop confidence in their political beliefs. And in art, John Wharton insists that instead of working "in a vacuum," his students must study buildings, paintings, and sculpture. After examining the relative functions of the academy and the church, of Athens and Jerusalem, DeVault and McIlhiney decided that the former is needed as the critic of the latter. They argue that students in a course on the New Testament should spend most of their time in a detailed study of the Gospels. For these teachers there is no conflict between content and method, no inconsistency between academic discipline and "discovery learning," between expository and inductive teaching, between facts and skills, facts and values.

In this student-centered education rooted in content students learn best, according to the writers, if the teaching is open-ended, a sophisticated blend of inductive and deductive processes. Rejecting the old reliance on didactic teaching, the authors recommend that the students be allowed to gather information and create generalizations inductively before using these generalizations deductively for additional learning. It is not surprising to find support for inductive learning among the humanists. "Discovery learning" has been in vogue in history classes for some time; open-ended classes have long been a staple of teaching in English. But Richard Brown proposes a novel use of inductive processes in teaching geometry. Instead of asking students to prove that a certain statement is correct, he asks them to prove whatever they can from given data. Instead of using theorems deductively to solve problems, students are asked to work together to create their own theorems. In a similar way Arthur Compton expects his class to create its own textbook instead of reading a standard text. Compton turns science teaching around by using class time for learning what was formerly taught in textbooks and using homework time for doing experiments.

A number of the essays explore detailed techniques for teaching a given discipline. A recurring theme is the belief that talented students must be allowed to move ahead at a rapid rate and not be held back by the lowest common denominator of the class. According to Kehl, "a stimulating pace" is indispensable to the teaching of French. Students who are intelligent enough to be studying calculus and *Hamlet* are not content to grind their way slowly through simple language texts. David Coffin insists that talented students in the classics be allowed to make "swift progress" through increasingly complex material in the classics, in some cases reaching Virgil before the end of the second year. Those authors who do not emphasize a rapid pace still insist that the material be appropriate for the talents of the students. Stretch athletes, says Kathy Nekton, beyond their own perceived limits. Do not teach students, says Rindfleisch, what they already know. These writers agree that work in the classrooms and on the playing fields be demanding.

Above all, our authors argue for a personal humanistic form of education and reject the utilitarian objective style that Dickens parodies in *Hard Times.* There is no Mr. M'Choakumchild teaching on these pages, no Mr. Gradgrind setting policy. In Nekton's essay on physical education she asks the teacher-coach to be more than a technician, to teach values as well as skills. Joseph Fellows and Jill Nooney point out that unless we care about the psychological well-being of talented students, they are unlikely to learn effectively. In the final essay Charles Terry argues that the goal of teachers should be to cultivate "determined charity" in the talented. He and other writers in this book believe that students should be educated in ways that will encourage them to care for others. Science, according to Arthur Compton, should be "science for citizens." If we deal with all sides of our students, if we guide them toward compassion as well as intelligence, if we help them gain confidence in themselves, then we will be teaching as we should. If we "respect the child," as Emerson puts it, we will best help him learn.

But this respect for students and this belief in learning rather than in teaching are not longstanding traditions. If this book had been written fifty years ago, it would have been a far different book, for Phillips Exeter Academy in 1930 was the quintessential old New England academy, a community in which everyone was measured daily and in which duty had precedence over desire. There was no question where authority lay. Teachers taught explicitly; students gathered information from their teachers or from their textbooks. Education at Exeter in those years was didactic not Socratic, cognitive not affective, institutional not personal, more Puritan than Unitarian. It was teaching more than learning.

Edward S. Harkness opened the way to change by presenting the Academy with a large grant of money in 1931. The Harkness Plan, which was based on small classes taught around an oval table, made possible a form of education far different from the model then in vogue at Exeter. If classes were small, then the teacher had little reason for relying on didactic teaching. If teaching veered toward the Socratic, then the institution would from time to time be less important than the personality of the individual student. Perhaps in time a new style of education would emerge that was less authoritarian than before. Perhaps learning would overtake teaching.

The Harkness Plan, furthermore, offered the faculty a chance to adopt the style of education envisioned by the founder John Phillips. In his deed of gift in 1781 Phillips told his teachers to care for the "morals" as well as the "minds" of their students. "Goodness without knowledge," he wrote, "is weak and feeble, yet knowledge without goodness is dangerous," and "both united form the noblest character; and lay the surest foundation of usefulness to mankind." Phillips was asking for a balanced form of education which would deal with the student morally as well as intellectually.

Ever since the first Harkness teachers began to arrive at the Academy, the faculty has been torn between the humanistic ideals of Phillips and Harkness and the stern tradition then in existence. Teaching began to change: it became less judgmental, less based on fear, less authoritarian, more inductive, and more concerned for the individual. But much of the old teaching lingered on. Even around the oval tables didactic teaching persisted; teachers still insisted that students gather large bodies of factual information; coverage of material often remained the end rather than the means of education. Teachers continued to concentrate on honing the verbal and numerical skills that good students brought to the Academy. In 1981 teaching at Exeter remains a blend of the old tradition and the Harkness ideal.

The seventeen teachers who prepared this book are asking their colleagues to turn more squarely toward humanistic ideals and to rely less on stern traditions. They are not asking teachers to give up content or to abandon expository teaching. They are asking them to dare to be flexible about the sort of content to be used, to blend Socratic teaching with expository, to rely more on the students than before, and to educate the whole person. They are asking them to think more of learning than of teaching. In Emerson's words they ask their peers to "respect" the "pupil" and in so doing show "respect" for themselves. That, they believe, is the way to teach talented students.

# I

*" . . . a continuing dialogue, a Socratic exploration."*

# ENGLISH

Norval W. Rindfleisch

ONE OF THE funniest and angriest scenes in the whole of Dickens occurs at the beginning of *Hard Times* when student number twenty, Sissy Jupe, is asked to define a horse. She loves horses, works with them every day in the circus, but, of course, she cannot come up with an acceptable definition, which is supplied by one Bitzer, the model student: "Quadruped. Graminivorous. Forty teeth, namely twenty-four grinders, four eye-teeth, and twelve incisive. Sheds coat in the spring; in marshy countries, sheds hoofs too . . . . ''

The question is asked by Thomas Gradgrind, successful capitalist and school inspector, who, with a government official, is examining the class of Mr. M'Choakumchild, a teacher recently mass-produced like so many pianoforte legs under the philosophic aegis of the utilitarians. Dickens is unmitigatingly vicious in his satire of the "murdering of innocence" that a purely quantitative approach to education has accomplished. Only Facts are allowed in education. Representations of flowers are not permitted on carpets; images of horses are not permitted on the wallpaper. Fancy and wonder along with feeling, compassion, beauty, and individuality are banished from the classroom and the lives of children. Sissy is hopelessly stupid, answering M'Choakumchild's questions about statistical survival and the greatest happiness for the greatest number by quoting the golden rule and expressing compassion for the relatives and friends of those who have drowned or burned to death according to the conditional circumstances of the questions.

What you sow also shall you reap, Dickens argues in the rest of the novel, and the consequences for Thomas Gradgrind's children are devastating. Sissy Jupe, fortunately, is too ignorant to get any Facts straight and is forced to drop out, or rather drift away, spared by her obtuseness from the dehumanizing effects of an impersonal school system.

Implicit in Dickens' satire is a positive philosophy of education. Be kind, Dickens tells us. Respect imagination, feeling, and sensitivity. Let learning be full of joy. Honor young people. Let them express themselves openly without ridicule. Let them be individuals with names, not numbers.

In the hypothetical atmosphere of Dickens' ideal educational setting, Sissy Jupe's response to the statistical rationalization of human suffering would serve as a point of departure rather than the conclusion of Sissy's education. Her response would be welcome in an English class at Phillips Exeter, for the members of the English Department have been for 50 years now committed with a vengeance to a personal, seminar method of teaching. In 1931, as a result of a gift from Edward Harkness, class size at Exeter was reduced to 12 students, and new buildings were erected and special tables constructed to institutionalize what remains today one of the most profoundly radical and responsible ideas in American education. The assumption that underlies the arrangement of 12 students and a teacher around an oval table is that each participant has special dignity, each deserves to be treated with respect. This respect is the cornerstone of true developmental learning. It precludes the implicit condescension of the lecture and the anonymity of quantitative evaluation. It entails continuing dialogue, Socratic exploration of content, often with the students asking and answering as many questions as the teacher. Like Socrates, the teacher is interested in mental processes, in the growth of the student as a thinking, feeling, changing human being, not simply in the student's ability to assimilate information.

The teacher must engage a broad register of qualities — the intellectual, moral, imaginative, social, and emotional — especially the English teacher, because the principal content of the classes is supplied by the likes of Shakespeare, Yeats, and Faulkner. The experience is more cooperative than competitive, though the possibility that a Socratic discussion will degenerate into verbal one-upmanship is the second most pressing anxiety of the seminar teacher. The first, of course, is that no one will say anything.

Such student-centered learning need not sacrifice standards. We seek to avoid the vacuity and glibness that often result from discussions without focused content. We want our students to share and appreciate our passion for ideas, form, and the best that has been felt and written. We do not believe that a dialectic can be conducted in a vacuum or that students can grow unless content is objectively or historically valid. We do, however, reject attempts to maintain standards through totally objective methods of evaluation. Our students read mature and difficult books and are expected to discuss or write about reading assignments daily. Long, objective tests are incompatible with the spirit of seminar teaching; our principal method of evaluation is writing. Our writing program has been integrated with reading; it is not conducted as a unilateral activity.

Despite the usual lament that most young people are invincibly ignorant and morally defective, the students who arrive hesitantly in our classes each September share several characteristics that make them particularly attractive to English teachers. First of all, most of them read with accuracy, sophistication and enjoyment. If they are able or talented in reading, it is enough. However, they bring other gifts that contribute to the genuine excitement and joy that occur so often in seminar classes.

Most of them were strong students at their previous schools and are highly motivated. They are, on the whole, hard workers, willing to pay the price for self-improvement. Most are outgoing and at least superficially amiable. Most have a healthy self-confidence and realistic self-esteem; some, unfortunately, can be arrogant and self-centered. Not surprisingly, we discover after a month or so that each has some special nonacademic talent. One girl may be a nationally ranked swimmer; a particularly shy and apparently immature boy turns out to be an expert on the defensive strategies of the Roman Legion. It is the purpose of our curriculum to challenge these young people, to make them reach, without destroying their self-confidence. It is easy enough to belittle and humiliate those who know less than we do. The effective teacher is one who can encourage students to take risks to the point of making mistakes without fear of ridicule.

The English courses designed to challenge such students are a little of everything: philosophy, linguistics, psychology, history, aesthetics, mythology, logic, grammar. The reading for each course is selected according to three primary principles: structural and technical complexity, maturity of content, and diversity of genre and form. In each course students read some poetry, short fiction, novels, plays and essays. Instructors are encouraged to select works from different historical periods, and not just from English and American literature. A tenth-grader, for example, might read and discuss *The Bridge over the River Kwai*, *Brave New World*, *Great Expectations*, *Huckleberry Finn*, *Inherit the Wind*, *Henry IV (Part I)*, *The Grapes of Wrath*, *Arms and the Man*, and selected poems of Housman, Hardy and Owen. A senior might read *Hamlet* or *Lear*, *Portrait of the Artist as a Young Man*, *Emma*, *Light in August*, *Fathers and Sons*, *Man and Superman* and selected poems of Donne, Hopkins, Yeats and Stevens.

Although emphasis may vary from course to course, the goals of instruction in each course remain the same: to teach reading and writing and the mental processes that underlie these basic skills — perception, cognition, imaginative manipulation. Each course is essentially the same, arranged in a spiral of graduated complexity and sophistication in the works read and the writing expected.

The approach is critical and analytical, not historical and biographical. Secondary sources are discouraged. The student is responsible for confronting a piece of literature on its own terms. The teacher guides students to consider a book's language, structure, themes and form: its power to move us to feel or think, to stimulate our imaginations. The goal is for students to develop sensitivity to a diversity of techniques, forms, rhetorical strategies and devices of language. Above all, the reading provides a wide range of vicarious experience as well as important social, moral and philosophical themes. We have been moved by Richard Wright's eloquent testimony in *Black Boy* to the emancipating power of reading. Books provided him with a vision of the possibility of things and the hope of an alternative destiny. The right books can also free even the economically advantaged from the deadly materialism of affluence.

Reading and class discussion become sources of inspiration for student writing. The seminar discussions serve as a rehearsal for the writing, and the writing experience reciprocally deepens the student's appreciation of craftsmanship and the power of the word. The critical approach provides a flexibility, a diversity and a range of reading experience more appropriate to developing adolescents than does the historical and biographical approach, which often results in hurried, desultory readings of works selected for deductive or other questionable reasons. The critical approach also permits a teacher to choose works on occasion for their relevance or topicality.

Teachers are guided by a reading list that reserves representative works for certain levels. *Crime and Punishment* and *Macbeth*, for example, are reserved for the latter half of eleventh grade and form the nucleus of a thematic cluster focused on citizens and the state. Teachers are free to organize their courses according to a wide range of secondary principles. Some organize according to a historical theme (such as the American Dream, in which students read *The American*, *The Great Gatsby*, *Death of a Salesman*, and *Native Son*, along with appropriate essays and poems), or philosophically — human fate, alienation, the existential condition — or morally. Some organize in a sequence or chain of pairings, mixing genres and forms in a series of connected ideas. Some intentionally avoid any programmatic arrangement.

Although each course might entail several secondary principles, the most important considerations remain that the works be of sufficient complexity, maturity and diversity to challenge students on each grade level. As this emphasis implies, we do not teach values directly, but in the books we read the authors deliberate and formulate all sorts of values — social, moral, religious, political — and our students discuss and write about them. We don't preach values; why should we, when we have Dostoevski and Fitzgerald and Dickens evangelizing for us?

If we in the English Department believe in seminar discussions with a vengeance, we believe in writing with a certain mystical awe.

Writing is more than a practical tool to convey information for professional self-promotion. It is epistemology, ontology and teleology. It is logic, rhetoric and poetics. Writing has emerged as the center of our English curriculum as the logical consequence of the seminar system of learning. In any school where teacher loads can be held under 60 students, conditions are ideal for a writing program to flourish; to do less, to fail to center a curriculum on writing with 12 students in a class, is to betray the needs of developing adolescents.

Writing is composing, and composing is a decisionmaking process of great complexity, even on the simplest level. It is more than grammar or spelling or punctuation. It is, above all, thinking, feeling, ordering, organizing. It evokes an inner sense of revision in most students, a mysterious power that continues to amaze teachers of writing who permit and encourage it to operate. Writing is also discovery, a mode of knowing. Students often find out what they really know by being forced to write; ideally they do not understand any content until they have written it. It is then, after a first draft, after they discover what they really want to say, that shaping toward form and correctness begins.

Just as reading is several times a more active learning tool than watching television, so is writing several times more effective than reading. What one reads has already been ordered, selected, evaluated. In writing, one must do the ordering, clarify the relation of ideas and the relative importance of evidence and arguments, select an effective rhetorical strategy, choose words for clarity, precision, and tone, select appropriately subordinate structures to mirror subordinate content.

One could argue that writing is an excellent preparation for life. Decisionmaking is certainly a transferable skill, if not a moral quality. Composition entails risks of error at every turn. The ability to acknowledge one's errors and accept responsibility for correcting them produces maturity. And frequent confrontation with that blank page — often daily — probably produces more moral courage than any playing field.

Our writing program is grounded in several general principles, some similar to those that underlie the developmental reading sequence. We expect diversity and growth in complexity in the writing our students produce. They write personal narratives, descriptions of people and places, fiction, drama, journalism, structural criticism, analytical, argumentative and reflective essays; obituaries, poetry, graduation speeches, letters to editors, intelligence reports, satire, character sketches, self-portraits, journals and college-entrance essays.

Students write from a variety of perspectives to a variety of audiences as they explore the voices that emerge within and as they begin to sense the importance of the world expanding beyond home and family. In each course we try to balance the teacher's insistence that students write about new ideas, using different techniques, with the students' right to explore their own subject matter and discover their own voice, perspective, or structure. Even when students are directed to experiment with a technique, the content is theirs.

We have three stages of emphasis for four-year students. Experiential writing dominates the first three semesters. Students write about the world around them — the given world of family, friends, school — in several modes, such as narrative, description, interior and dramatic monologue, and dialogue. Although students are asked to write frequently — especially in class — about their reading, most of their papers are based on personal experience so that they develop self-confidence as authors. Each student becomes an expert, writing as a professional to the teacher and fellow students rather than as a hesitant amateur, as often occurs when students are required to write exclusively about a narrow range of literary topics they neither fully understand nor care about for a teacher who has studied the material for several years in college and graduate school. A sense of authorship develops more effectively when the writer has leverage on the reader.

During the middle semesters emphasis is placed on moving students from participant-writer to observer-writer, from self-awareness to audience awareness. It is during these semesters that students learn about the writer as mediator, arbiter and guide. We encourage students to fictionalize more objectively, to use ''I'' as a device of fiction rather than simply as an expression of self. Students experiment with different voices. They are required to reach beyond personal experience and explore or investigate other peoples' worlds and interests.

This stage of development as writers corresponds to the emergence in many students of a second self with whom each holds private, often critical, discourse. This complex and critical stage of growth is too often characterized simply as refinement of ''cognitive'' skills. It is much more complicated than that. We require students to write papers in which the skills of explanation and analysis are balanced with skills of narration, description and characterization. The reporter-at-large, the family-heritage paper, multiple-perspective fiction, intelligence or reconnaissance reports, college-entrance essays, third-person self-evaluations and policy statements or editorials are all representative assignments during tenth and eleventh grade.

In the latter half of eleventh grade and throughout the senior year, the emphasis shifts to the intellectual. Students write longer analytical and interpretive papers. In fiction, we expect them to handle anonymous narration and more complex narrative time schemes. We also focus on maturity of style, but earlier skills are not abandoned. Students still write personal narratives and poetry. Sensitivity to detail, perception, and convincing dialogue are still important. They have not been superseded by cognitive skills, as though literary criticism were some higher form of expression. No one in his right mind thinks that the critical essay is superior to the short story as a literary form.

We defer intellectual emphasis for two reasons. Beginning writers develop a surer sense of who they are as authors by writing initially about personal experience. Second, after several semesters of reading and classroom discussions of literature, students develop greater self-confidence as well as an appropriate vocabulary for handling more abstract and intellectualized papers. Sophisticated cognitive skills seem to develop later than experiential skills in most students.

Through this sequence, we attempt to integrate reading and writing. Students are assigned to write a paper using a specific technique (an eyewitness point of view or the present tense, for example) after the class discusses its use in a novel or short story. More often then not, free papers are inspired by a book or a class discussion. A novel such as *Native Son* might provoke several completely different papers in any one class: an essay on rats or the color white, a statement about social justice, a philosophic dialogue about power, a description of a limiting or entrapping environment. It might also produce a critical assessment of the last third of the book. Writing is better when students read works similar in theme or form to what they are expected to write. The story of Bigger Thomas becomes a moving, vicarious experience for most of our students. They are better informed; their sense of fairness and social justice is deepened. They become more profoundly human, and they become better writers.

Perhaps reading is our most effective teacher of writing. Generations of great writers have testified that their own development was influenced by writers they admired. Reading books does not interfere with developing a natural or personal voice. We do not use works of literature as models to be slavishly imitated. We might use fiction to inspire a poem; an essay might produce a short story, a novel, a play; any form can evoke a critical or reflective essay.

Nothing interferes more with the growth of young people, than an environment devoid of the well-written word — the worlds of television and careless oral language, which often produce derivative content, clichés of thought and expression, vague diction, and limited syntactic variety in student writing. Reading and writing reinforce each other as skills when the connections between them, especially on the level of craft, are clarified.

In teaching writing we believe in the "basics," but our basic principles are only tangentially related to those promulgated today in the "back to basics" movement. By basics we do not mean drill in grammar with canned sentences in exercise workbooks or memorizing grammatical nomenclature. We have not instituted remedial writing courses labeled "competence," for we well know that competence is an issue in every paper—not an eternal condition of the soul mastered in a single semester. Syntactic, semantic and rehetorical competence in tenth grade can be syntactic, semantic, and rhetorical failure in twelfth grade. Because writing is perhaps the most complex of all human activities, making errors goes with the territory. Errors gradually disappear only over a long period of constant and frequent correction.

Many of the following basic practices and attitudes that permit our students to become writers are logical extensions of seminar teaching. Most have been validated by recent research.

1/ Students learn to write by writing, frequently, in various modes, and to a variety of audiences. The teacher may use supplemental aids such as diagnostic grammar tests, grammar texts, workbooks, vocabulary sheets, or sentence-combining exercises, but not to the extent that any of these becomes a substitute for student writing.

2/ Students are encouraged to write about their own experience. They choose to write about books, their feelings, relatives, special interests, political passions, and what they may have done last summer, which in this permissive age is one of the most interesting papers teachers read.

3/ Grammar and style are taught most effectively by noting errors in the student's own writing and by requiring the student to correct the errors. We often select examples of writing problems from a set of student papers and duplicate and pass them out to the class for collective consideration. Stylistically we encourage students to write economically and concretely. It is an axiom of our writing program not to teach students what they already know as revealed by what they are writing correctly.

4/ Evaluations of student papers are positive as well as negative, promptly returned, and open to student counter-response and eventual dialogue. Students should see noted errors as opportunities for improvement rather than as justification of a grade. Covering a paper with red marks is not always productive.

5/ Students read their papers aloud in class for reactions and encouragement. The teacher should not be the sole audience for student writing. Conferences between the student and the teacher are expected, often while the student is searching for a topic, writing a paper or doing a revision. Writing is rewriting, also. The teacher's advice is most useful while the student is making decisions rather than after.

6/ Teachers of writing should practice writing and be willing to write along with their students or to share first drafts of their own compositions with students.

Given our obsession with reading and writing, we have abandoned several of the goals and functions of a traditional English department; some we disavow enthusiastically, others reluctantly. We do not aspire to replicate ourselves by cloning English majors with courses that duplicate our own university educations. We do not aspire to produce establishment professionals—doctors, lawyers, bankers—though we do believe that our general program in reading and writing is an essential precondition of effective use of the specialized language of the professions.

We are obviously not content to produce mere linguistic and mechanical competence through drill so that our students may write flawless letters of application in the job market, for we know that grammatically correct writing can be insipid. We have no special interest in the history of literature or in relevance or moral earnestness or the relation between knowledge and goodness, though we value each as a resource in the development of reading and writing skills.

The traditional conception of English as a service department of other disciplines does not obtain. Our faculty has agreed for half a century that each department should teach reading and writing in its area. Indeed, we consider the other departments as service departments for English. Our students are better able to organize their papers because of their training in mathematics. We appreciate the sense of history that emerges in our upper-division students as a result of the efforts of the History Department. We are also grateful to the History Department for assuming the burden of teaching students documentation and footnote procedures. The Classical and Modern Language departments do an excellent job of identifying and explaining grammatical nomenclature. The training offered by the Science Department in inductive thinking is particularly useful as students grope for revealing generalizations and supporting evidence in interpreting literature. We welcome the skills and content of the other disciplines as students' allies in confronting the written word and shaping written works.

Seminar teaching is a system of learning in which, theoretically and if all goes well, the teacher is seen less as an authoritarian and more as an adviser, consultant, and editor. In actual practice we teach far more than we should. We talk too much, we grade too heavily, we are too impatient with superficial responses. We work too hard to elicit a response from everyone. We find ourselves often asking question after question, none of which seems to strike a resounding chord in the minds of our bewildered students. And then there are times when we ask the one question that begins a series of brilliant exchanges among our students, illuminating a passage in *Lear* or a scene in *The Sun Also Rises.* Then we know that we understand that passage and scene as we have never understood them before.

We are authorities whether we want to be or not. We are older, we have read more. We must judge students' academic performances with grades and their behavior with disciplinary action. Students perceive us as authority figures even when we try not to be. Some students are even disappointed when we spare the red pen on an early draft of a paper. They expect us to criticize them. They would also like us to do their work for them, supply them with the right answer. And so we must resist students' natural and very human attempt to define our functions in their terms. Seminar teachers in particular must be ever wary of the leverage that age and experience and maturity have given them.

Teaching in secondary school is different from college and graduate school teaching in one profound way: at the university the student becomes a disciple of a Great Person. The secondary school teacher around the seminar table enjoys no such special status and must prove himself each day in each class. If he rides his own academic hobbyhorse in class, the passionate focus of his intellectual maturity, he should do so infrequently. To expect sixteen-year-olds to ride the teacher's hobbyhorse is outrageous. In secondary school it is the teacher who must respond to the students' special interests, or his comments on student papers will lack credibility. It is the teacher who must read Tolkien or Hesse or Vonnegut or Ayn Rand, or Barth and Barthelme in order to participate knowledgeably in class discussions, for students frequently cite in their observations unorthodox books, bizarre activities, and strange encounters of the transcendental kind. The teacher as specialist has no place in the English classroom, though he or she must have a specialist's knowledge of the workings of literature and the composing process to survive.

We must resist the natural impulse to direct all our attention to those bright, attractive, talented and responsive students who make our classes go. We must also resist spending most of our time (usually at the expense of the friendship of the majority of students, who don't seem to need us so desperately) rescuing from anguish those few who cry to us in pain. English teachers are especially privy to secret griefs, real or imagined, that surface so often in papers. We owe each student equal time and interest, even the hostile and unpleasant young men and women who openly dislike us.

Our attitudes are as important as our methods. We must begin each semester with a sense of adventure, with our willingness to try new books and writing assignments and to renew the wonder of our own educations by trying out with our students some neglected classic we have not read since graduate school. We must enter each class with an enthusiastic commitment to the usefulness of that hour, with a concern for our students, and a love of what we teach.

We must celebrate each day the concrete word, the sacred whatness of revealing detail, the glory of the simple sentence, for our students too readily abstract and intellectualize. We must bite back the cutting remark, knowing that what we perceive as haughty indifference in a student's manner may be only a mask to cover fatigue. Perhaps these attitudes even more than our principles will influence our students' intellectual, emotional and moral growth. We will never know, however, for we lack reliable proof of our abiding presence.

Like all teachers, English teachers have an anxiety that underlies every relationship, every paper, every discussion. Do we teach this student better with criticism or encouragement, judgment or mercy? We worry that our notation of errors may prove too destructive. We worry that we are being conned by a baleful look and an apocryphal tale of woe.

Sometimes we feel a kinship with the judgmental spirit of Flannery O'Connor, who, in her wonderful perversity, places in the mouth of the Misfit in "A Good Man is Hard To Find" her most recurring theological theme. After shooting the grandmother, whose selfishness and pride delivered her and her family to the terrible fate that awaited them on a Georgia roadside, the Misfit says, "She would of been a good woman, if it had been somebody there to shoot her every minute of her life." We feel like the Misfit when confronted by a particularly bad set of papers, suspecting that their errors proceed from moral depravity or disrespect. We pounce on the papers and angrily scar them with our red pens, believing that only continuous criticism will stop the errors.

At other times, however, we are moved by the redemptive spirit of Dostoevski, who tells us in *Crime and Punishment* that human nature is instinctively good. Look, he tells us, Raskolnikov befriended Marmeladov, gave money for the funeral, and protected the girl from the lecher. Only his erring and arrogant intellect got him into trouble. Have patience, he tells us. *Have faith in the self-correcting powers of the human soul.* At these moments we realize that if we are patient and allow the students to correct their errors and rewrite their papers, their pride of authorship will emerge. Like Porfiry Petrovich, the ultimate seminar teacher, we must allow the process of self-correction to take place. If we do, our students may then realize a self-sustaining grace of style and intellect to go their own ways.

# RELIGION

Mary T. DeVault
David B. McIlhiney

TERTULLIAN'S QUESTION, "What has Athens to do with Jerusalem, the academy to do with the church?" is not one that the founders of early independent schools would have asked. To John Phillips, the founder of Phillips Exeter Academy, the relation between religion and the intellect was clear: his school was to be a theological foundation, her instructors were to be practicing Congregationalists, and the knowledge they taught was always to be subservient to "virtue and true piety." If in her early years the Academy did not quite live up to her founder's vision, neither did she stray significantly from his principles. Biblical training was assumed, church attendance was enforced, and no local family was permitted to accept student boarders unless it practiced "the daily worship of God." When the first Instructor in Divinity was appointed in 1817, the founder's hopes would seem to have been fulfilled.

Yet it was to be just over a century before the appointment of another divinity instructor. During most of the intervening years, the instructors inculcated piety through example and precept, but religion was not a part of the formal curriculum. After biblical courses were reintroduced, however — and even more clearly when the Department of Religion was formed in 1958 — Tertullian's question became a real one for the Academy and for other academies as well. The old orthodoxies — Calvinist and others — had long since eroded, and faculties no less than students began to reflect the pluralism of national schools. There were some who questioned the legitimacy of teaching religion at all, others who questioned how to approach that study.

Departments of Religion have a choice between two models. The first, the confessional model, owes more to the church than to the academy. It would have the instructors teach only a particular religious tradition as true, expecting that most students would conform to that doctrine and piety. This model has at least the advantage of clarity, but by its failure to take seriously the questionings of adolescents from diverse backgrounds, it is suited only to homogeneous schools that maintain explicit church or synagogue ties.

The second model is a scholarly one. This would require the instructors to suspend their own theological commitments in order to teach only about religion, without interjecting their own judgments. This model, a common one among university departments, has the appeal of both clarity and scholarly integrity. In schools that have adopted it, the instructors usually maintain no formal connection with the chaplain, who may, indeed, teach in some other department. But this model has its own weaknesses. In the first place, it can inhibit teachers from responding openly and completely to their material. As Peter Slater remarked: "It is an irony of the times that philosophers and historians tend to preach at will to their students, while religion professors are supposed to remain scrupulously noncommittal."[1] Further, to isolate the teaching from the practice of religion may be to impoverish both. History provides many examples of an arid scholasticism divorced from the lives of believers, just as our own era is demonstrating the dangers of an evangelical faith that rejects its own scholarly roots as well as free intellectual inquiry.

It is possible, however, to blend characteristics of both models. At Exeter, for example, the five department members reflect a considerable variety of denominational commitments, ranging from Pentecostal to Roman Catholic. Collectively we serve as the school's chaplains, while individually we are encouraged to express our differing theological views in our classes, taking great pains to present our material objectively. Sometimes, of course, the very nature of the material evokes change and commitment in particular students. We attempt to treat such experiences with respect but not to seek them. To do

1. Claude Welch, ed., *Religion in the Undergraduate Curriculum*, (Washington, D.C., Association of American Colleges, 1972), p. 33.

so in the classroom would, we believe, violate the spirit of our teaching.

The model is not a neat one, for there remains within it a distinct tension between religious scholarship and the ministry. The tension becomes acute when an academically weak student who believes that he has grown in a religion class is disappointed by his grade. Those are the times when teachers long for a simpler, clearer model to guide their work. Yet the tension can also be exciting, for it can awaken students not only to a religious dimension in themselves, but also to the connection between their classroom studies and the way they choose to live their own lives. As E. Harris Harbison wrote: "If the age of the Reformation is a fair example, conscious tension between love of learning and devotion to Christ is a sign of health and vitality in the Christian tradition rather than the reverse."[2]

Exeter's Department of Religion currently offers more than a dozen courses, loosely grouped under the headings of scripture, theology, ethics, comparative religion, and philosophy. Approximately half of our enrollment is in the area of biblical studies, where we undertake to provide a close scrutiny of either the Hebrew or the Christian scriptures for our students, most of whom have had little previous acquaintance with the biblical materials. Other than scripture, our most popular course is ethics, in which we try to confront students not only with personal decisionmaking but also with such larger issues as genetic engineering, political morality, and world hunger. In this course we require students to read *The New York Times* to encounter the range of ethical issues our society faces. Students frequently respond that this course has helped break down the barrier between the classroom and what they imagine to be the "real life" that awaits them beyond school.

The method we use in all our courses grows directly out of the Harkness system of teaching. Perhaps we can best illustrate it by describing our introductory New Testament course. To study this literature successfully, we believe the student must confront the mind of the biblical authors, understand the circumstances of their society, and identify their purposes in writing.

2. E. Harris Harbison, *The Christian Scholar in the Age of Reformation* (New York, Scribners, 1956), p. 166.

The approach is simple. We begin with the text itself, usually the Gospel of Mark, analyzing it carefully, chapter by chapter. The student first outlines the action of a single chapter, and then, after studying it as a whole, attempts to write an interpretation focusing upon why Mark groups together a particular combination of passages. Why, for example, does Mark in chapter eight have the feeding of the multitude, followed in turn by the Pharisees' request for a sign in Dalmanutha, the disciples' missing the meaning of the feeding, the healing of the blind man at Bethsaida, Peter's confession, the first Passion prediction, and the proclamation about taking up one's cross and losing one's life?

The student's struggle with Mark's combination of these passages leads him gradually into questions that reveal Mark's broader theological perspective. Typical examples of such questions are: Why are the disciples continually so obtuse, even Peter at the climactic moment of his confession? Why does the second feeding story come so soon again after its introduction in chapter six? As the student continues, further questions will arise. For example, the healing of the blind Bartimaeus in chapter nine often evokes the question: has this something to do with the blind man in chapter eight? Is Mark again using his characteristic "sandwich" technique to reveal an important insight?

The central aspect of this study is the daily journal in which the student records the action of each chapter and his subsequent interpretation. The teacher reads these journals each night in order to point out observations not supported by the text and to encourage thoughtful analysis. As the term proceeds the teacher can watch the students come to constantly greater sophistication in their understanding of what Mark is communicating. Since the student's reflection grows out of his daily journalkeeping, it is imperative that his theories be constantly evaluated for substance and validity.

Throughout the course, the text is always the discipline. When a student presents an interpretation, other students will often challenge it and request that he support his view from the text. Merely pious or hackneyed statements begin to fade, and the substance of Mark's theology begins to emerge. Because the students discover Mark's underlying message on their own, interest remains keen and class discussions have a high level of both enthusiasm and participation. Students are eager to know if their readings of particular passages will be confirmed by their classmates. A special moment happens, in this process of pooling ideas, when the class as a whole reaches a startling fresh insight. Each student knows that on a particular day it could be his contribution that will become the key in this joint effort.

The course can be equally exciting for the teacher. No two classes are similar, even when they are studying identical material. The line of student questioning will vary, and insights will be reached by different routes. One of the most fulfilling experiences for the teacher comes when a student suggests an original hypothesis to illuminate an old problem. Continuing refinement, continuing depth of questioning, continuing demand for new interpretations happen to the teacher no less than the student.

Once the students have learned to read theologically through the study of Mark, they are ready to move on to the rest of the New Testament. We usually go from Mark directly to Luke because Luke's theology develops so logically from Mark's, but occasionally follow with Matthew for the sake of contrast. As soon as students become familiar with more than one gospel they are prepared to deal with the life of Jesus in an entirely different way. They have begun to see that they are studying not the biography of a historical person, Jesus, but the theological interpretation of a particular author who is trying to relate the meaning of Jesus' life to his own human experience. The students no longer concentrate upon isolated, often moralistic statements; they begin to realize that they can no more see Mark's Jesus through one verse or passage in Mark's gospel than they can comprehend Shakespeare's Othello through one line or scene in Shakespeare's play. Increasingly the students will not be disturbed that Mark's Jesus is very different from John's, or that John's perception of the resurrection is radically different from Luke's. The students see that they are confronting the varied attempts of different human authors to explore a mystery. The conflicting images and differing perceptions of the various authors can lead to a fuller realization of that mystery. This is a demanding but mature approach to the study of scripture.

It may appear at first that this method is entirely inductive, but such is not the case. Much expository teaching is necessary throughout the course. Questions concerning sources, oral tradition, geography, first-century culture and history all arise from the students' study of the text itself. The teacher is constantly presenting this background as the questions arise. Information about Old Testament references, the significance of Greek vocabulary, or pertinent ideas from modern scholarship are woven into the class discussions daily, just as would be true in a lecture course. The distinctiveness of this method is that since the teacher cannot be certain when the knowledge may be called for, he must be ready at any time to be a source of enriching or necessary background. Student questions determine when and what information will be given.

Once the students have learned to analyze the New Testament by looking for the author's purpose, they are ready to read what contemporary exegetes are writing about the same material. At times the students will disagree with the scholars. At other times their insights will give the students support in defending their own hypotheses. It is enjoyable to observe a student when he discovers that a scholar's interpretation concurs with his own: "I found that out for myself!"

Another important resource is contemporary literature. For example, following the study of Mark's gospel, students frequently read C.S. Lewis' *The Lion, the Witch, and the Wardrobe*. Students are genuinely delighted when they discover Lewis' rich symbolism, so similar in many ways to the symbolism of the New Testament. In most disciplines the student learns to think in literal, linear patterns, with clear distinctions between cause and effect. It is impossible to explore adequately the content of the New Testament using such thought patterns, for the truth contained in this literature remains stubbornly in the realm of mystery. Scripture communicates itself through suggestion rather than definition. To understand this literature requires that the student gain facility in what could be called the language of intuition — symbolism.

Doing textual analysis around the Harkness table is an ideal way to teach scripture. The search is open-ended. The joy of discovery is real. In the simple integrity of seeking the author's intent, the text reveals a power of its own. The Jewish student, who often understands the person of Jesus with a depth unknown to many Christians, confronts the very enigma of the New Testament. The Christian student, who has taken Christ for granted through the layers of his inherited tradition, confronts a new radicalism in Christ's message. However, it is the response of the unbeliever that is often most impressive as one observes this student treat the material with increasing seriousness and reverence. It is here that Athens challenges Jerusalem to greater appreciation for the gift which has been entrusted to it.

We come back, then, to Tertullian's question, to the tension that lies at the heart of our teaching. As believers, our loyalty is to Jerusalem; as scholars, we owe more to Athens. But when we watch the unbelieving student intently examining the literature of religion, seriously exploring what the author understood and why, we see that Athens can give Jerusalem a new integrity. It is the respect of the nonbeliever who acknowledges the authenticity of something he cannot accept that challenges the person of faith to greater thoughtfulness and reverence. Athens is the often gentle but persistent critic of Jerusalem's claims.

# DRAMA

Donald P. Schultz

THE BASIC ASSUMPTION in teaching drama is the importance of individuals working as a group. As a result of the work of Konstantin Stanislavsky, theatrical productions are now perceived as united ventures blending the best efforts of experts trained in specific areas. Individual professional development is not ignored: actors learn to act, directors learn to direct, designers learn to design. But each has to integrate his work with that of the others so that the production becomes a unified whole rather than merely the sum of the individual contributions. And on stage individual actors have to learn to react to other actors, to work cooperatively rather than as individual stars.

The Stanislavsky method has important implications for the teaching of drama. Since all who participate in a production must be familiar with the work of the others, the student of drama has to learn a broad variety of skills; ideally students should be trained as actors, directors, designers, technicians, and playwrights. With the emphasis on the group rather than on the individual, students have to be taught to work with others. The approach in the dramatic classroom has to be as cooperative as that on the stage.

To instill the attitudes and values of individual effort in a cooperative venture, the best way to start is to include individual students in the process. The students must be made aware of the goals and aims of the various exercises at the time they are being asked to learn them. They must develop a sense of trust that will enable them to experiment with their minds and bodies in useful ways. They must have the sense that others will not criticize them destructively, that the group will be working to improve the result. They must be able to critique the work of others, knowing all the while that their own work will be critiqued. In the end students must have a sense of personal reward for the cooperative work they have put forth.

In order to accomplish these goals and give as many as possible the chance to participate, a drama program should include both curricular and extracurricular activities. These two are often distinct. At Exeter, for example, the curricular offerings are teacher-designed, while the extracurricular are on the whole student-designed and student-controlled. Students clean the building, take care of minor maintenance, supervise workshops, organize touring groups — in short, they are given important responsibilities. But even though different, the two types of activities are blended together to create an integrated program. In the student workshops, for example, the students practice the same skills that are taught in the regular curriculum.

The main emphasis of the curricular program is on acting, which is taught in a sequence of three courses. We also offer courses in elements of theater design and playwriting, but these are rather specialized courses for a small number of students. Acting is the focus of the curricular program because on the stage the actor is the focus of attention. Writers will write better plays if they have some appreciation of the problems faced by an actor. Designers will design better if they understand the physical limitations imposed by good acting. And directors will be better directors if they understand how an actor works.

In the courses on acting we teach that acting is not merely a technique, not simply repeating learned responses. Instead it is a reaction to what happens on stage, and it comes from within the actor. In the process the students learn a great deal about themselves as they begin to understand the mental and physical tools that they possess. We try to stretch the imagination, to loosen the body, to help students feel emotion, seeing it in others and understanding it.

In the introductory course, offered at the tenth- and eleventh-grade levels, we start with the individual but always with an eye to helping him fit into the whole. Students spend much of their time in the early weeks in exercises designed to build confidence and to establish trust in the group because a willingness to try must be instilled early if there is to be hope of success. Further along, the course uses various exercises to teach the students about themselves, how to use the senses and the body in a coordinated way to produce an emotion or action. Finally, the students progress to playing improvisational scenes.

Some of the exercises that help to develop these tools are sensory awareness "games." In one, the student sits alone in a darkened dormitory room for several minutes listening intently, and then reports to the class what he has heard. In another exercise, visual acuteness or the sense of touch may be used. Concentration exercises teach students that they can isolate their thought process from actions around them, that they can operate in a way that focuses on an objective not shared by others in the same room. All of these develop important skills and techniques to be used later when an actor must live and act within the limits of a given character in a play.

Another group of exercises is designed to stimulate the imagination and to bring about an interaction of physical and mental activity. In one elementary transformation exercise one student leads by pretending to engage in a simple physical activity (chopping wood with an ax). A second student joins and emulates the motion; then the first student sits and the new leader transforms the motion into a new action with similar elements but based on a different idea (throwing a ball). So it goes around the class — the ball becomes a snowball, and the act of gathering snow becomes that of building snowmen. In this activity each student must concentrate intently since he may be next. He must understand what is in the leader's mind without a spoken word, and when asked to participate must call up from memory a different action that uses elements of the previous motion.

By the end of the course students progress to improvisational scenes. After a topic is given, a scene or setting described and the characters identified, each actor at a command must play a part. The lines spoken are the actor's own and the emotional response comes from his interaction with others on stage. As skill develops these scenes can be good teaching and learning tools. In one three-character scene all agree at the start that they are at home in the afternoon, that one is the mother, another a seventeen-year-old son and the last is a twelve-year-old daughter. This much is jointly known, but only the mother will know that she has had a tough day, that dad called to say that he will be late for supper. Only the son will know that it is very important that he have a private talk with dad. Only the daughter will know that she has been invited over to a friend's house as soon as she can get there after supper. The opening line is given, "Johnny, will you take out the garbage?" Each actor must now react to another's improvised lines with the sort of response that his character would give with his particular cares. The exercise pulls together many elements that have been worked on during the prior weeks. Mother's subtext, the unspoken thought on her mind, colors the way she speaks to Johnny, who must respond to the mother's tone as well as her words. And the daughter must pursue her objective, to get supper finished as soon as possible. At the end of the scene all participants, actors, teacher and student audience, engage in a lively critique, which often becomes a review of the material studied earlier in the course.

At no time in this beginning course do we allow students to work from a script because we do not believe that they can use a script until they have developed the physical and mental tools necessary to bring characters to life. They must learn to expand on the written word, to endow it with living examples of their own, for only then can they act.

In the intermediate course, which relies on the written word, eleventh- and twelfth-grade students study scenes that are selected from plays presented in their historical setting. During the semester a student will study plays in a chronological sequence beginning with Greek drama and progressing to modern American drama. Although the course is selective, we attempt to give students a sense of the evolution of style and structure in a historic frame. The course is team taught, and the students are tested in conventional ways.

At the beginning of each week a lecture is given to the entire group by either of the two instructors. The goal is to help students understand the way in which playwrights in the past have solved problems in writing that the students will also have to face. The middle of the week finds the students in small working groups developing short eight-to-ten-minute plays of their own. Each student gets feedback as all students comment on the others' work, and the teacher is only one member of an active group working to improve the product. At the end of the week the students perform short scenes from the plays assigned for the lecture. They take turns directing each other in order to gain experience in interpreting another author's work. The experience sharpens their ears, eyes and imaginations as they wrestle with the problems of giving meaning to the thought in the script. Students not performing watch with a critical eye and after each scene participate in the critique, which follows the pattern used in all of our courses. Since we assume competence and a variety of interpretations, simple declaratory statements expressing opinions about the performance are not allowed and all comments have to be phrased as questions. As a result of this technique the door is opened to experimentation—even to something as extreme as a well-reasoned defense of playing Hamlet as a clown. The technique allows the trust established early in the course to continue—and with it the development of new ideas.

For a limited number of second semester seniors who have had training in our program, or its equivalent, we offer a seminar in acting. The students in this course are given advanced work in exercises similar to those taught in the introductory course but with an emphasis on emotional recall, transference and physical training. After previously learned skills are polished, the class as an ensemble begins to work on a production. In cooperation with the Physical Education Department, students are excused from their sports commitment and instead take part in a series of physical exercises useful to actors. About one-third of the class time is devoted to physical instruction that ranges from warmup exercises to dance. Since the course is designed for those who have more than a casual interest in drama, the students are given work that is often taught in professional acting schools.

The students enrolled in these academic courses are greatly outnumbered by those who take part in the extracurricular program. Those who teach in the department consider this extracurricular work just as important as the theater courses and find the teaching every bit as demanding and rewarding as that in the traditional classroom. The program has three branches: school plays (or major productions), workshop productions, and minicourses. The major productions are similar to the traditional dramatic programs of the last several decades. Although the extracurricular program stresses the role of the students, the major productions are faculty directed (often with two directors) and usually have faculty members in key production positions. In this way teachers of drama are given the opportunity to develop their own professional skills just as art teachers paint or sculpt and music teachers play an instrument. The system also enables the professionals to blend their efforts with those of the students in producing the unified production that is desired. Tryouts are open; actors need not to be experienced. Students act as crew heads and work on the production staff. The rehearsal period is short and intense, usually about twelve hours a week for four weeks. The discipline of the rehearsals has become such a tradition that students come prepared to work. Each play develops its own élan, experimentation is the rule in the early going, and teaching techniques are designed to help the actors approach their roles. The faculty feels an obligation to do one "classic" play each year, but otherwise the range of productions is broad. About 150 students participate in the four major plays either as actors or backstage, but only a half dozen or so play more than one major role in the course of a year. The major productions are the showcase of our best efforts as a faculty-student cooperative effort.

The minicourse part of the extracurricular program, which sometimes enrolls as many as the formal courses, originated from student demand. Some minicourses—often on technical aspects of the theater—are offered more than once a year and may have a sequential development that leads to advanced work. Others are taught only once every two or three years. Standard offerings include lighting, stagecraft, play reviewing, makeup, and publicity; there are less frequent offerings in costume construction and play analysis of a particular period such as Theater of The Absurd. The courses are taught by the regular faculty with occasional help from more advanced students. Although there are no grades and no credit is given, class attendance is required and there may be examinations. The courses usually meet once a week and last for eight to ten weeks. While students use the program to improve skills or to satisfy curiosity, the faculty uses it to try out material for the expansion of the regular curriculum. The first minicourse, more than a decade ago, was a direct forerunner of the introductory and advanced courses in acting. Present interest in minicourses in technical theater suggests that more advanced work in that field will find its way into the regular curriculum.

The workshops are the heart of the extracurricular program and the best example of student involvement. Students run the show; they act, direct and produce as many as twenty-five plays a year, ranging from excerpts from classic drama to original productions. Rehearsals are limited to a total of ten to twelve hours over a two-week period; the goal is not a polished production but rather the opportunity for students to practice skills learned in other parts of the theater program. It is a place to experiment, for a student to try and perhaps fail without a major penalty, a place where student leadership emerges, a place where students teach students, a vital component in our philosophy of theater education. Although some students work only in the workshop program, most often the workshops provide a steady stream of students into the minicourses and the regular courses.

In drama, as in any discipline there is a body of information to be learned, but it is the process that is important. Both teacher and student must share the burden of teaching and learning in an active manner. Each must trust the other to listen with understanding, to share in experimentation, and finally to critique with compassion. Students must see that they can teach as well as learn, teachers must see that they can learn as well as teach. When the process works at its best, education becomes a rewarding experience for all.

# II

*". . .it is the content that offers the setting."*

# HISTORY

E. Arthur Gilcreast

> *For a man without history is almost in the literal sense half-witted. He is only in command of a part even of his own mind. He does not know what half his own words mean, or what half his own actions signify.*
>
> G.K. Chesterton

IN HIS USUAL pugnacious way Chesterton goes to the heart of the matter with his tribute to history. Since the present is but a fleeting moment and we know not what the future holds, all we really have is the past, that rich treasure house of data, stories, situations, personalities, and values, the combined memory of mankind. Just as men or women without memories, amnesia victims, stand helpless, unable to comprehend the world around them, so too groups and nations without history are rootless, without a past and with little understanding of the present. They are, in Chesterton's words, "half-witted."

Heavy, then, is the responsibility of history teachers in deciding what to teach from the past and how to teach it. Not the least of their problems is that they have so much competition, for novelists, preachers, politicians, dictators, men and women on the streets all dispense their brand of history. And the people love it; Americans today, for example, show a remarkable appetite for historical novels, genealogical roots, and antiquarian objects. We all reach out for our past so that we can know where we are today. The task of the history teacher seems an easy one: simply tap the great reservoir of the past and give our students what they are asking for — the story of the past.

And yet all is not well. Despite the great enthusiasm for history, enrollments in history courses declined in colleges and schools during the past two decades. And despite all the history being taught in novels and on the television screens, students do not seem to have learned as much as we would like. They do not have a deep understanding of their roots, their institutions, and their traditions; they lack conviction in their values and their beliefs; they are — in Chesterton's words — only partly "in command" of their "own mind[s]."

This combination of a love of history and a lack of conviction presents history teachers with great opportunity — and an important duty. Their task is to help students turn their passion for history into conviction by introducing them to situations that present the great issues that have challenged men and their institutions. They must confront students with real people making decisions in real situations in the past — Pericles leading Athens into war with Sparta, Henry VIII breaking with the Roman Church, James Madison defending the Constitution of the United States. In the process of reading what these leaders said and what others said about them students will begin to appreciate what goes into making a decision. Even more important, students should then have the chance to take their own stand — with Pericles or against him — and hold their ground against others in the class who may not agree. Then it is that students will confront values and sentiments that will test the validity of their own experience and their own reason. And finally — the hardest task of all — students will be asked to present their views in writing with conviction. With this sort of experience students may begin to "know" what much more than half their "own words mean."

In the process skills will be learned. Students will learn to ask the clever questions that help them uncover meaning from past words and events. They must search for data, facts, and somehow learn how to evaluate the evidence, how to sort it out, how to keep certain facts and forget others. They will identify people and places, define terms, arrange facts in chronological order. They will produce sentences, then combine them into paragraphs, always moving steadily toward the major task of turning facts into generalization. The teaching of skills is an inevitable part of studying real people in real situations.

But more important than the skills is the content, for it is the latter that will excite students and make history meaningful in their education. It is the content in *Roots* or *War and Remembrance* that attracted viewers and readers by the millions. It is the content that is more fun than learning how to write a topic sentence. And it is the content that offers the setting for enabling students to develop conviction about their values and beliefs — the real end of the study of history.

To promote this end, the teacher must take a strong hand in helping students identify the broad themes that they should trace in their reading and class discussion. In American History, for example, there is the tension between the authority of the central government and the rights of individuals or sections. At the outset, the instructor must frequently summarize what has been accomplished in the previous class and forecast what will be the focus of the class ahead. At longer intervals, a broad overview of the themes covered from the very beginning reminds the students where they have been and points the direction of future inquiry.

Unless the teacher builds the students' confidence in their ability to get within the issues, to see the values and sentiments underlying them, and to esteem their own opinions on them, the students will forever remain outside the exciting process by which history is made. They become mere spectators who can be conditioned to parrot responses, but they cannot become thinking participants in the study of the past or the formation of the future. Textbooks inundate students with factual material. Without confidence in the themes of the story, students cannot discriminate on the importance of factual information. The weak students surrender to the volume of information and their minds go blank; the better students add to their confusion by conscientiously attempting to learn everything equally well.

The study of Hamilton and Jefferson in the 1790s offers teachers a good opportunity to allow students to judge important issues. The history of this era confronts students with facts ranging from economic data about the assumption of state debts and the funding of the national debt to the details of diplomacy in the Citizen Genêt affair. These facts are of no use and interest to modern teenagers unless they understand that the major issue at stake was nothing less than the definition of what sort of political system the new nation was to adopt. Once alerted to an awareness of the issues, students can try to decide on the relevance of various facts to the generalizations they are in the process of developing. Students will already have some opinions on these generalizations because the issues of what is a judicious extent of government planning or how involved Americans should get in foreign affairs are still debatable today. As the testing of these opinions takes place, many students will find themselves almost as concerned as Federalists or Republicans over the outcome. The measure of the student's success is his personal reaction to this process. Most students come alive because of it, and for even the slowest student the experience is an important beginning in independent thinking.

There would be no justification for the small size of classes if teaching was wholly expository; thirty students would be as acceptable as thirteen if all speaking was done by the instructor. Fifteen students is probably the upper limit if each student is to do some talking, for the success of a discussion class is directly proportional to the amount of student participation. Since not all student comment is likely to be enlightened, the chief aim of discussions is to build students' confidence in their ability to speak in the presence of others. The task is a challenging one because students fear nothing more than the disapproval or mirth of their peers and they are too willing to defer to those few who are orally confident. The discipline of history provides some protection against this danger of a few students dominating discussion.

When personal opinion and broad generalization might go on interminably, the factual content of the daily assignment provides sharp limits to any comment — or so it should if students have the courage to challenge and question. It is indispensable, therefore, that the teacher establish immediately an atmosphere conducive to challenge and contradiction, insisting all the while on the distinction between challenging another's arguments and insulting his person. Though courtesy prevails, no argument is safe from challenge — especially that of the instructor. The teacher should vary the type of positions he takes on the issues so that students can get confidence, and even pleasure, in opposing his views. Such inconsistency need not be mere dissimulation if the teacher clearly expresses his true views at some point in the class or later in the course. They should receive no less criticism then because by that time students will have confidently taken firm stands of their own.

Conclusions aside, the point of the dicussions is to organize facts and develop generalizations. Often the "answer" is not reached until the end of class, if at all. What happens along the way is all important; students say what is on their minds, they martial the facts, they try generalization even if only to find that they do not persuade others. They gain confidence that they have worthwhile opinions that others will listen to; they learn that the inability to persuade others is not a failure but merely a temporary setback. They learn to persist. While my own method is to develop toughness in the students by frequently challenging what they say, other instructors emphasize different techniques. The most patient ones build confidence in students by showing infinite consideration for what they say, helping the individual to build something substantial from some part of what he has said. Teaching is a matter of personality, and students learn because of their experiences with a variety of teachers.

The other side of the seminar experience — the ability to listen — is much more difficult to cultivate. Students are rarely as persuaded by what their peers say as by what they say themselves or by what the teacher pronounces (another reason for the teacher's inconsistency in class discussions). Try as they may to be attentive to the comments of others, students are not very discerning about language or the implications of what is said. The source of the problem is that students are inept at identifying the assumptions implicit in arguments. It is one of the chief tasks of the discussion to encourage listening and to develop confidence and skill in analyzing oral arguments. The teacher sets the example by aggressively listening to what the student is saying; not to rule on what is correct but to discern what the student is trying to say and to locate some premise in the comment that can be used to expand the discussion. Second, since student comments are seldom predictable, the teacher must be flexible about the direction of the day's discussion so as to avoid rejecting a comment as off the topic. It is easy enough to turn the discussion eventually into the planned path.

Let's imagine that the teacher requests comments on Alexander Hamilton. The student states that he admires Hamilton because he was "smart." Not much to work with really. But go on. "What do you mean by smart?" The teacher asks. "Well, Hamilton seemed to know what he was doing; he had some ideas about how to make the country a better place." "In other words," the teacher helps out, "you admire Hamilton because he was a true leader, a man with plans for the country, rather than a man who simply followed what the people wanted?'' By expanding on what the student has said the teacher has dignified a weak comment and perhaps shown the student how to say it more strongly and clearly next time.

The teacher turns to another student, preferably to one who seems little interested in what has happened thus far. ''Do you agree, Bill?'' Bill typically allows that the answer he has heard seems agreeable to him. The teacher now has at least three directions in which to proceed. He can ask Bill to describe the most important Hamiltonian plans (the factual route), or he can ask Bill to explain why Jefferson could possibly be critical of Hamilton (introducing a second generalization), or he can try to awaken Bill by asking him why he has so little confidence in democracy as to prefer the plans of a monarchist over the will of the people (the adversary route in which the teacher assumes the role of Jefferson without saying so). What follows depends on Bill and on the reactions of other students. Further discussion may focus on the abstraction of leadership vs. democracy, or it may get into the Hamiltonian program to test its merits as planning. Whatever the order, the class eventually discusses the facts, the philosophical positions of Hamilton and Jefferson, and the merits of leadership vs. democracy in the modern world. Students identify their assumptions, and those of others, about the nature of man, the role of government, and the proper operation of the political system. The dry facts on assumption, funding, and the Bank of the United States become essential weapons for the students as they strive to persuade others. The method is useful because some history is learned, and it is fun because an ongoing game of matching wits is being played.

An education based on talking and listening, then, aims to build the confidence of the student in handling facts and generalizations. All classes begin with one of the two and work toward the development of the other. Little formal note need be taken of historiographical literature and controversy, but the instructor must be aware of the major interpretative approaches so as to offer various generalizations in class discussions. Marx, Turner, Beard, Hofstadter, and New Leftists may be mentioned during the course, but only as their viewpoints spring naturally from the content of history. It is not wise to ask novice students to evaluate or compare major historians or schools of historical interpretation.

In addition to class discussion, instructors should also employ other exercises to familiarize students with the resources of history and to develop their confidence in using them. Primary sources should be assigned along with textbook or monographic reading on any period of history. These can be used to challenge interpretive skills and the ability to make a generalization. Instructors should assign a good deal of writing in the form of short papers, hour examinations, and quizzes — perhaps a minimum of once a week. And in the advanced courses students should write a longer research paper based in large part on primary sources. The results of independent research are often mediocre at first because students lack the overview needed to place primary sources in perspective, and because they do not have the benefit of class discussion and critical argument to clarify the meaning of these sources. But the experience is useful, and the subject of the term paper will often be remembered far longer than most topics studied in the daily assignments. In each of the exercises the principles involved are the same as those sought in class discussions. The process of critical thinking and the confidence to think independently are at the heart of the matter.

Teachers can use courses in the social sciences in the same way as history courses. A business course, which employs the case study method, gives the teacher another opportunity to use critical questioning to build student self-confidence. Since the material of the business course is contemporary, the seniors taking the course feel familiar with it because of their previous newspaper reading. In addition, the case studies are complete in themselves; all the factual evidence is present, the focus is on a single situation. Accordingly, discussions are often spirited. The area of disagreement is over assumptions about the objectives to be achieved in solving the business problems. These assumptions alone give meaning to the solution proposed and justify making certain facts more important than others. Students will often differ about what are realistic objectives, and this exercise in judgment, in the application and advocacy of values becomes the focus of discussion. Having studied and criticized the assumptions of Hamilton, Jefferson, and others in American History, students receive in the business course a logical extension of their analytical training as they strive to construct their own programs for action. Since there are no right answers, the student is limited only by the ability to persuade and to utilize pertinent factual evidence. Seldom is any solution to a case entirely satisfying or without some drawback. Students learn to give up something in order to achieve other ends, and they discover that the application of their own values to the situation has consequences for other people, the company, and society as a whole.

Whatever the history or social science course, nothing develops conviction about values more convincingly than the application of the ideas to real people in real situations. Ideas have consequences, and when those consequences are carefully identified and critically examined, students soon discover that there are fundamental values, acceptable and unacceptable results. It is this refinement of the sensibilities of youth that ought to be the real end of education. The young can be easily conditioned; with their powerful memories for facts, their emphasis on experience, their poorly developed assumptions about themselves and their society, they can go about far too long — as Chesterton wrote — "half-witted." An education based on talking and listening treats students as mature equals and cultivates those tender shoots of value and sentiment developing in them.

# ART

## John Wharton

> *. . . we are asked to teach visual literacy and a sensory* language.
> *Language and literacy refer to words and nothing else. The*
> *metaphor that applies them to artistic matters is false and*
> *misleading; it destroys the case for art, whose rightful claim to*
> *special merit is that it is a mode of thought without words,* inar-
> ticulate, sui generis. [1]
>
> Jacques Barzun, "Art and Educational Inflation"

THE MODE OF THOUGHT to which Barzun refers in his perceptive essay on the necessity of art as a part of basic education is
the focus for any syllabus or teaching approach in the studio.
As any visual art teacher will affirm, however, this mode,
like most things attitudinal, is not easily defined. Unlike
other academic disciplines that teach well-defined, logical
processes, art demands of its students a slow accumulation of
intuitive responses. The best an art teacher can do is to lead
students through exercises and discussions which explain
and develop techniques, promote ingenuity, give pride in
craftsmanship, and provide the base upon which a lasting interest in the visual world can be built. In short, the students
must engender within themselves a critical sixth sense about
what they see and what they make to be seen.

This critical acuity is, of course, developed through decision
making. Every time a student, or an artist for that matter, ap-
plies color to a canvas, defines an edge with a line on paper, or
models a form, decisions are made. Initially these decisions
must be conscious and carefully justified; eventually they
become intuitive. The progression is similar to that in which
fluency in a foreign language is achieved to the point that the
speaker is no longer fully conscious of grammatical structure.
Once this happens in art, Barzun's "mode of thought" is opera-
tional.

---

1. Jacques Barzun, "Art and Educational Inflation," *Occasional Paper 25*
(Washington, D.C., Council for Basic Education, 1979), p. 9.

There are neither textbooks nor teachers' guides that aid this process in the visual arts. In an educational age of laboratory materials, mathematics texts and answer books, collections of historical documents, and books that purport to explain and teach both the sound and sense of poetry, this lack of art textbooks may come as a surprise. If so, you may have some inkling of both the excitement of teaching art and the academic suspicion with which many institutions treat their art departments. Without a set syllabus to fall back on and without measurement devices to determine success, the art teacher is at the same time the creator of his own program and the victim of other people's misunderstanding of it.

In order, then, for secondary school art teachers to devise a pedagogy that will be successful in the studio, they have to do two things. First, they must accept the fact that a large part of their teaching is going to be remedial. Second, they must determine how they can most effectively help students achieve the visual and critical fluency mentioned earlier. The first is relatively simple, if often personally frustrating; the second is exceedingly complex.

To understand why an art teacher's work is most usually remedial it is necessary to see the overall pattern of most students' education. There is a terrible moment for most children in primary school. Having been encouraged to draw and paint and manipulate clay, the great majority find out suddenly that, although their visual products adorn the refrigerator doors of their parents' kitchens and the windows of their classrooms on national holidays, no one takes their efforts seriously. Writing, reading, and manipulation of numbers become the tools for survival and the emphasis on the teaching and learning of them all-consuming. When children bring home something they have made and of which they are proud, their parents may praise them for the expressive ability that they suspect most children have. An A on a civics test, however, not only brings praise but also triggers that future-vision part of parenting — "perhaps my child will go to law school."

Once the child senses this double standard, and most sense it quickly, the interest in making or talking about art rapidly diminishes. Thus, from the age of six or seven until they take an art course in high school, college, or nowhere at all, most students think of whatever art education they receive as being predominantly peripheral. It should be no shock to visual arts teachers when they give their first assignments to have a large percentage of their classes say that they cannot draw. (Would they ever tell an English teacher that they could not write or an algebra teacher that they could not add?)

The schools themselves have been little help in correcting this educational deficiency. Although it is generally understood that all disciplines, academic and athletic, take time, intensive practice, and commitment to achieve proficiency, this belief has not been applied to art. The amount of time which a student is required to spend in an English classroom or on the playing fields, for example, in order to receive a high school diploma when compared to that required in the art studio or art history classroom makes the discrepancy abundantly clear.

In order to explain this attitude towards the teaching of art a great deal of emphasis has been given to the notion of talent. Art, it is popularly thought, is produced by talented, self-taught artists, who are tempered by economic privation and who work only when inspiration has them in its grip. On the one hand, this view of the artist is harmless, romantic nonsense; on the other, it has been extremely detrimental to the development of art education. For, if the education of Picasso or Michelangelo, for example, is conveniently forgotten, then the necessity for art education as a whole can be ignored. Talent, if it truly exists, cannot flower without education nor can it easily survive in an atmosphere that does not provide a fundamental continuum of learning.

Thus, the art teacher's first priority in the studio is to take students who, for the most part, have been deprived of visual education and attempt to build in them self-confidence, concern for the visual world, and a sense of normalcy when working in the studio. It is the kind of therapy at which most of us, from time to time, have thrown up our hands in despair. Only when we understand that our only option is to believe that art and Barzun's "mode of thought" cannot be taught and that this option is not acceptable, do we perceive our job as what it really is. With this understanding there comes, in the best of art teachers, the development of a missionary zeal, which often disconcerts our colleagues and is written off as defensive insecurity.

In addition to confidence the teacher must also develop a pattern of active, visual thought in students. As pointed out earlier, no standard methods for producing this development exist. The result is that the teaching of art has often gone to extremes in its quest for a successful approach. At one extreme is what might be called "the-resident-genius-artist" method. Here the teacher accepts the students into his *atelier*, gives them some words of fatherly advice, and then allows his genius to rub off on them as he indoctrinates them with his own style. This method is a direct result of the success of Renaissance apprenticeships and the fact that we do not remember its failures. Its flaw, of course, is that today students expect to produce their own work and not simply paint in the skies of their teacher's masterworks. As a result, once the effect of the pied-piper personality of the teacher wears off, the student is left floundering. The dedicated ones sometimes survive through persistence and belief, but the questioning students are usually ignored and quickly shrivel.

At the other extreme is the diagrammatic approach in which the teacher leads the students through endless exercises. Line weight, texture, mass, color relationships, and all the other seemingly simple elements are taught separately and abstractly. The assumption is, that once students understand the basic techniques, then art will appear full-blown from their hands. On the surface, such an approach seems logically attractive, but it lacks the crucial ingredient of decision making.

Let me outline one teaching method that avoids both the pitfalls of dependency on teacher personality and of emphasis on hermetic academicism. The project is not a new one and, although most usually used in sculpture and architecture classes, can be adapted to any number of different media and disciplines, anything, in fact, that ends up with a purely visual product. An eager and excited class can take it to remarkable levels of sophistication while a less inspired one can still understand what has been learned by going through the required processes. If it sounds simple in its description, rest assured that it is not in practice. Because of its initial, apparent simplicity the project does not threaten students and, once they are involved, gives them few escape routes. The problem is called "The Seven Stones."

The introduction of the project is crucial. The students must be presented with all seven steps of the process so they have some idea of the logical progression, are made aware of the quality, both of thinking and of product, that is expected of them, and are reassured that there is a certain degree of latitude for self-expression within the various stages.

The students are first asked to collect seven stones or pebbles that can easily be carried around with them. They must base their choice of stones upon visual and not metaphorical criteria. Color, texture, or similarity of shape are adequate reasons for choosing; that a stone looks like a tropical fish or that the six small stones are the followers of the one large stone are not acceptable reasons. The students must be able to justify their choices to the class and the teacher. Thus, the first step in visual decision making is taken.

For the second part students are required to produce seven sheets of drawings. In each case the subject is one or more of the pebbles.

1. A simple outline drawing without shading or texture.
2. An enlarged detail that emphasizes the texture.
3. A contour drawing with the addition of shadow(s) cast by raked lighting.
4. A three-dimensional, "realistic" drawing.
5. A drawing including another common object that indicates the relative size of the stone(s) to the viewer.
6. For architectural students: a plan and several elevations.
   For sculpture students: a drawing of the same stone(s) done from several different viewpoints.
7. A contour drawing with watercolor applied to approximate the stone as closely as possible.

In many ways these drawings are the basis of the entire project. Through them students learn that drawing is the universal symbology of art. They must be able to recreate what they see in both their real and mind's eye. Accurate and sensitive drawings supersede language, and the students begin to approach Barzun's "inarticulate mode of thought."

This second step after the initial choice of pebbles is usually the most time-consuming and painstaking. Students have to be convinced that each of the seven drawings must stand by itself as a visual product without the necessity of direct comparison with its subject. The teacher must insist that the students consider carefully the placement of the image on the sheet, the scale of the image in relation to the size of the page, the choice of viewpoint and medium, and the "finished" quality of the work.

The next two steps of the project are carried out simultaneously. As homework, the students are asked to build a cardboard box which will hold an inch of white sand in which the seven stones are eventually placed. The teacher discusses scale, structure, material, types of glue, and color before setting the students free to begin construction. Few students, for example, remember the weight of a given volume of sand even though they learned it on the beach when they filled up their first buckets as small children. Few have ever constructed a box or thought about why most boxes have four sides and a bottom rather than five sides and a bottom. For most students this part of the project is their first indication that art often has to deal with practicality and that form, function, and structure are symbiotic.

The fourth step must be a discussion of the visual relationship of objects as it has occurred in the history of art because the fifth step will be the arrangement of the pebbles in the sand. The students need to know that they are not working in a vacuum and that the decisions that they will be making in the placement of the stones are similar to those which artists and architects have been wrestling with for thousands of years. The Athenian Acropolis and Agora, the Roman Forum, the medieval walled city, the University of Virginia, and Soleri's Arcosanti help students understand space relationships and the underlying requirements of function. Romanesque façades and the volumetric massing of Gothic cathedrals begin to explain to students the expressive elements that can be involved in spatial organization. Michelangelo's Medici tombs, Rodin's *Burghers of Calais*, Henry Moore's figure groups, and the multiple figures of George Segal indicate the importance of careful placement in multipart sculpture. Finally, slides of Japanese gardens and the contemporary work of Carl André, Richard Serra, Isamu Noguchi, and others show how functional requirements and figurative gestures have been abstracted.

Now, equipped with some historical perspective, the students arrange their stones in the boxes of sand. They are urged to experiment, to question every placement, to use the fluidity of the sand, and not to decide upon a final arrangement until they feel that they have explored innumerable possibilities. At this stage they are given little advice and guidance but know that the sixth step, the critique, will help them decide whether to keep or change what they have done.

All the students and the teacher participate in the project in terms of the decision-making process they have gone through. It is vital that students and teacher ask questions and make comments that are supportive and not pejorative. Visual justifications and descriptions that the whole class can see as they look at the arrangement are the only ones allowed. The exhibiting student may refer to the drawings and to art-historical precedent but must always focus on the product at hand. Responses to questions such as "Oh, I dunno, I like it that way" or "This represents the sun, and these smaller ones, the stars" will not do.

The end point of the critique is to support the students' ideas and choices as well as to stimulate change and refinement. In many ways it is the most difficult part of the project since it comes closest to violating Barzun's "*in*articulate" base for art. Students find it easy to talk about art in a literary way. They can most easily describe what they see by alluding to common visual images: "It looks like a cow" or "The arrangement of stones looks like a mountain chain." But they must be dissuaded from this. Such use of common images dilutes the uniqueness of the constructed form.

Even though the students may learn, as they should, that the oral language of art is severely limited, they must struggle to develop precise, visual responses. The teacher must encourage statements such as: "The impetus for the design was to achieve a sense of balance. Thus the pebbles are massed so that there is a balance between the few dark ones that appear heavier and the large number of lighter colored stones." Further, and perhaps even more important, students must learn that they are pursuing similar, difficult goals which can be shared orally and visually.

Since the combination of the sand and stones is not permanent, and since product can be more reassuring than process to most students, the last part of the project is making a final form using many of the skills, insights, and ideas they have learned. For architecture students this may mean plans and elevations, perspective drawings, or other kinds of renderings. It may even result in the stones transformed into buildings. For sculpture students it may call for a reproduction of the stone arrangement in clay or wood, or a development in welded steel or cast metal. As with the earlier drawings, the finished object must have its own presence divorced from what it represents. If it is possible to combine the terms, it must have a "small monumentality."

All of this may seem like a great deal of time and trouble to spend on and with seven stones. Yet the process simulates in rather a simplified way the modes of thought and manual creation which all artists go through. If the student has taken the project seriously, and if the teacher has used that alchemical combination of humor, sympathy, and rigor which encourages that seriousness, then the student's sense of space and the objects within that space will be considerably heightened.

From the initial, visual choice the student has progressed through elementary drawing techniques, construction methods, historical reference, verbalization of the process, and the production of a final, unique form. He will have sampled enough of Barzun's "mode of thought," that joyous isolation of decision making, to begin to make instinctive, visual choices. This is not to claim that the student has now learned everything or that all he needs to do is to repeat the process of the seven stones project simply substituting people, buildings, or trees. But it is a first step in the rekindling of an interest in the visual world, a regeneration of an excitement dulled by societal inhibition.

General, basic education is the business of the secondary school. Part of that education must be to heighten visual perception, to provide the historical background that will allow intelligent, visual choice, and to foster pride in manual accomplishment. Only an infinitesimal number of students will continue their studies in the visual arts and make them a lifelong concern. They will come across increasingly sophisticated language and technique whether it be in art history or in the making of sculpture. However, drawing, visual relationships, and references to the past will remain central through their careers.

For those students who do not continue in the visual arts, secondary school art courses may be even more important than for those who do. Even a modicum of visual thinking may determine one day what kind of house or style of furniture they buy, or whether to support their local art museum. As with choices made by students of political history, we must all live with the results.

Many art teachers would deplore this goal of sensitizing the next generation as being too general and crassly modest. But if our visual environment improves through widespread public interest, then we have achieved a great deal, and if we promote a climate in which artists and architects flourish, then we have performed a formidable task. The day, in fact, could come when the names and works of important visual artists were generally known and visual choice, based on Barzun's "mode of thought," was second nature.

# III

*"...an unending process of investigation"*

# SCIENCE

## C. Arthur Compton

THERE IS SOMETHING about nature that inspires a sense of wonder, even awe. Things that creep or crawl, chirp or squeak, flit or wiggle, the stars and the endless dance of the ocean waters have entranced young people since the earliest recorded times. Children find their natural world exciting, mystifying, perhaps frightening, but always beautiful. Some respond by capturing nature on canvas or in rhyme; others merely look and enjoy. A few elect to study natural phenomena formally; these we call scientists. They set out to order the chaos of impressions and experiences and from that ordering comes a measure of predictability, even of control. One function of a school science program must be to introduce students to the possibilities of this kind of intellectual commitment.

Another function is to contribute to the needs of citizens, for in our society everyone must make decisions that require technical information. Since few individuals can ever have all the experience or knowledge they need to make informed decisions, society must rely upon the collective wisdom of its members. We adjust our behavior according to the advice of authorities in areas in which we are ignorant. Responsible citizenship involves the critical selection of those whose advice is to be accepted. Because many of the decisions that face modern industrial society are technical in origin and substance, citizens need to be exposed to the nature and limitations of the sciences, and must be familiar with the character of scientific evidence if they are to behave rationally and responsibly in a complex world.

Several assumptions can be made in teaching able students. First, students with ability are likely to be self-motivated. They will have aspirations, perhaps for college, perhaps for a creative or professional life. Second, most students will not elect science as a profession. We should not approach our classes as if they were filled with striving young scientists. Finally, these young people will do well in whatever courses they take. Those that want, or need, factual information will surely obtain it in abundance in later courses or through reading, while those who neither want nor need such information will just as surely forget or misremember it. The task is not to provide a plethora of scientific information but to create a sense of excitement over both the prospect of learning and the inherent power of disciplined curiosity.

If teachers accept these assumptions, they should resist the trend toward individualized programmed instruction. And if all the students are reasonably able, then heterogeneous sectioning is preferable to homogeneous sectioning by ability. True, there is ample evidence that students learn at different rates. If the intent of the course is to cover material as rapidly as possible, then students should work at the different rates that their maturity and ability dictate. Individualized instruction or homogeneous sections have their place in such professionally oriented instruction. They have no place, however, if the teacher believes that introductory science should serve a more humanizing function than the preparation of young technicians, and that this function is as important for the future scientist as for the layman.

On this basis the primary concern in class is to convey the more social and less individual aspects of the sciences. The excitement generated by experiences in the laboratory or among the reference books demands communication with others, and it is in the ensuing debate where new ideas are hesitantly presented, challenged, defended, revised, perhaps discarded, but ultimately reinforced and expanded that students really begin to understand as well as experience the human enterprise called science. How sad that many students think that science is what they find in a textbook! How unfortunate that the public perceives open disagreement among scientists as evidence of uncertainty and even weakness in the scientific process! Such debate is a necessary part of science and is fundamental if science is to progress. Scientists, at least the good ones, will learn about this part of science by becoming embroiled in it, but how do the laymen learn? They do so by becoming involved at their level, and that is what these classes must provide.

Students must be challenged to articulate ideas clearly; they must be encouraged to criticize, defend, disagree, refine and then repeat the process. These are the crucial methods of science that citizens must come to understand as clearly as must the scientists, but these aspects are never conveyed in the science textbooks or the precanned experiments of the laboratory manuals.

We are all buffeted by information and should recognize that data can be presented in different ways for different purposes. Graphs, words, charts, equations, pictures, all can be used to present information, but so also can they be used to misrepresent and distort. Where do students learn the techniques for presenting data, for recognizing distortions? Who is to challenge the media's motives, if not the science teacher, when news releases about nuclear reactors dramatize the cooling towers, which are irrelevant to the nuclear controversy but whose unsightliness is surely persuasive? Where do students learn that shifts in the coordinates on a graph can produce apparently contradictory pictures of the same data? Facts do not speak for themselves, pictures do not always tell a true story. Statistics can be made to lie, and in our participatory society are too often made to do so by those whose eagerness to advocate exceeds their desire to clarify. This is the world our students must cope with, and our task is to make them more effective. Surely such issues are ripe for consideration in a science class, but they are never found in the science textbooks.

With able students a textbook is no longer necessary in introductory physics. With the less mature students in the first semester of the course, it may serve some purposes: to provide an organized outline, a battery of exercises, and a few problems. But it can be abandoned in the second semester. Colleagues have not always agreed that the course can be adequately given without a text, but in England the Nuffield Physics project revised school science education entirely without producing any texts at all. Books are not useful in science teaching any more. They tend to control the syllabi and emphasize The Word — the very antithesis of science. And they tend increasingly to be written for students whose reading levels are such as to suggest they should not be taking any science at all. Able students need a better challenge than that. I prefer to sit my students in a semicircle and pace around, poking my finger at individuals as I try to draw ideas from the students themselves. We develop our "text" in class with arm waving and demonstrations and laboratory experiments where possible, and we draw upon the experiences of the students, not some remote author whose views may have been obscured by an overzealous publisher.

Not everything has changed. We still use problem sets as homework to give practice in those manipulative skills our educational system encourages so outrageously. We still have tests and quizzes. Some students have a reference book they can turn to on their own; others use the library. But we develop our ideas together, and since we are not sectioned homogeneously, we come to recognize that each can contribute one way or another. That is as it should be, for no one person has a monopoly on wisdom. Surely it is more important for the gifted science students to learn this from their less able classmates than to get one course farther up the professional ladder. They will climb ladders in college, but they may lose sight of their partnership in humanity along the way unless we help them in the secondary school to seek a wider vision than just another course in science.

The process of extracting information from our experience in class and defining our ideas together rather than lifting them precanned from a book takes time. Because there is still some premium placed on the coverage of materials that may be included in national testing programs, that time must be created somehow from within the present schedule of classes. One way to find the time is to use the weekly laboratory period as another class session. My students now do their experiments on their own time, as homework, in an open laboratory. This one shift has made all the difference and has begun to change what is expected of the students, and of the teacher.

In assigning a laboratory experiment the teacher hands out direction sheets and gives the students a week to perform the experiment and prepare a report. The directions are deliberately barely adequate; they do not provide a recipe to be followed mindlessly. Much of the design and establishment of procedure should be left to the student, for that is where the experiment becomes personal and a creative experience. So the teacher provides fewer clues than formerly about how much data to take, what range of values to investigate. The student must decide such things either through preliminary calculations or trial and error. Since the laboratory is open outside of as well as during class hours, including evenings, the student cannot assume that the supervisor will be a physics instructor who can provide help. Indeed, the physics student may be surrounded by biologists dissecting their foetal pigs. In time, perhaps we will encourage some artists to use the laboratory as a studio. These are not distractions. They are open acknowledgement that there is a unity to the human experience and that no one discipline has the unique view of reality.

There are hidden traps in these laboratory procedures, both for the student and the instructor. Data can easily be faked when students are not under direct observation and control; we must deal with intellectual dishonesty as firmly as we can. The experiments are not as routine as they once were. Some will serve primarily to confirm ideas already discussed in class, but others will serve to introduce new ideas, including some even the teacher may not anticipate. The teacher can no longer outline steps of the experimental procedure, prescribe amounts, or even preselect the proper equipment. These steps were taken before in order to insure that the students could complete their tasks within the scheduled laboratory period. Now, the only limit imposed on students is the time their interests generate as they pursue new ideas. Because the instructor can no longer be sure what the students are doing or finding, there is a new premium on clarity of communication in the reports. The concern is less with the achievement of some preconceived result than with the process of disciplined study of a phenomenon, any phenomenon. The question "Is this answer close enough?" no longer has any meaning; students do not ask it any more. But the students will have trouble getting used to the implications of these new procedures. They will want to know when they are finished, which means that they are still thinking in terms of a closed experiment rather than an unending process of investigation. The only answer to the question "When will I know if I am done?" has to be "When you are satisfied."

There are mechanical problems with an open laboratory. Broken equipment, concerns for safety, these and other issues can be handled. There may be penalties; some instructors have to work extra hours to supervise, occasionally in the evenings. But there are advantages as well, including a need for less duplication of equipment because whole classes no longer perform the work at the same time. The approach will be a success when students begin to argue in class over whose interpretation is right and when the unexpected becomes the routine. When such results occur, teachers will know that their students realize there is more to science than recipes and formulas and specialized manipulative skills that can be tested either by a science department or by national testing agencies.

In this new sort of physics course students will learn more than did their earlier counterparts about the nature of the scientific enterprise. But the class will cover far fewer routine facts than it used to. There are whole areas of the traditional syllabus that will never be touched at all. Fortunately, these omissions have not significantly changed the scores of able students on the College Board examinations. Perhaps it is because the students are able that the teacher can get away with this tinkering with the subjects covered by the course.

There are further changes to be made. One of the leaders of science curricular reform in Great Britain recently suggested to an international conference of school science teachers that there are three levels in science education. First, there is pure science, "science for the inquiring mind" as he put it, which he depicted as a triangle. "We have had a lovely time inside that triangle," he said, "searching for clues, evidence, and encouraging critical thought." Outside that triangle is a square, which he called "science for action." Pure science may tell about the laws for circular motion, but how you bank a curve in a road involves science for action. Occasionally we try to make science more relevant by taking sorties out into the square, but we have so enjoyed ourselves that we have ignored the fact that outside the square is a third aspect to science that is so multifaceted that it can only be depicted by a circle.

This circle represents "science for citizens." The world is filled with problems that demand technical input, and although science and technology cannot provide answers to these problems, they will not be resolved without technical input. Societal problems do not have unique solutions although most school courses, including science, have notoriously emphasized the fiction that every question has a single answer. Nor has man yet learned the basic lessons of ecology and thermodynamics: it is impossible to do nothing and it is not possible to do just one thing. Every action will produce some benefits, but at some costs. In reality, then, there are no answers, only alternatives. Science defines those alternatives and suggests what some of the benefits and costs may be. Technology increases the variety of alternatives that are available and economically viable. But society must decide whether the benefits outweight the costs and hence must establish priorities among the possibilities, and it does so in accord with philosophies or codes of ethics that lie beyond the scope of science to define. The discriminating citizen helps set those priorities. Governments determine whether differences of opinion will be resolved by totalitarian or by democratic means, by rule of law or rule of force, by reconciliation or through compromise. Our quality of life is not determined by science, but our way of life surely is limited to what is possible within the framework of natural law. In our science courses we help students learn about natural law, but we seldom bother to suggest how technical information can, or should, be used in the affairs of men.

So there is more to science than we have been teaching in our classes. If we are concerned with helping students become effective members of society, we must venture into that "circle" and consider ways in which science, or the scientific attitude, can enhance our way of life. We must find the time, even if at the expense of topics long held dear by science teachers. We must be prepared to discuss at length issues and beliefs, some of them touchy in nature, perhaps, that are not yet a part of any national testing program. Teaching able, motivated students should mean above all that it is possible to take a few plunges with impunity. These students will do well regardless of what we do in our classes. So the real question is whether teachers have the nerve to overcome their inertia and the comfort of the familiar and explore new areas and new techniques in science teaching with students who are strong enough to stand against the tyranny of tests and textbooks.

Fifteen years from now I will look back from retirement. Maybe I will see that the students with whom I have been trying these ideas have become wiser and more effective adults than did those I taught before. That is something to look forward to with hope and growing excitement; so I had better get on with my experiment.

# MATHEMATICS

Richard G. Brown

A MAJOR GOAL of mathematics teaching is the involvement of our students in the personal process of discovering mathematical ideas and formulating problems. The student who parrots textbook proofs and formulas without understanding them may never know the joy of mathematics. But the student who uses educated guesses to solve a problem or to judge whether another student's hunch is correct is committing himself or herself to an often exhilarating process. This process of an inductive leap followed by a deductive argument has been used for centuries.

No subject is better designed for the application of these principles than geometry. It is quickly apparent to students beginning a geometry course that the subject is much different from previous mathematics courses. There are no elaborate arithmetic problems, no polynomials to factor, and few equations to solve. And most different of all is geometric proof, where the solution is not a neat number or algebraic expression that can be underlined and labelled "ANSWER." These differences in themselves take time to get used to, but there is another reason why proof is difficult for many. To illustrate, consider a standard original proof:

*Given:* $\angle 1 = \angle 2$
$\angle 3 = \angle 4$

*Prove:* $\angle 7 = \angle 8$

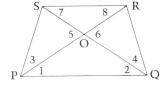

Here the student must invent a chain of deductions to arrive at the specific conclusion ($\angle 7 = \angle 8$) of his teacher or textbook author. For some students, this proof has too many steps, and, while none of the steps is itself very difficult, the whole chain of steps is a bit overwhelming.

On the other hand if the teacher erased what was to be proved and asked students to decide for themselves what *they* could prove from the given information, the whole exercise would change from the teacher's problem or the book's problem to the students' problem. The second process is far more fun than the first, and even slower students can enjoy success because they can generally prove *something*. It may be that PO = QO in the exercise above or that $\angle 5 = \angle 6$. From these observations, other deductions follow until the class together has proved that there are congruent triangles and parallel lines. As the students quickly learn the deductive process of building on the deductions of others, the class discussion is likely to become animated.

Here is an example that shows that erasing the "Prove" of an exercise can be used early in a geometry course, even before congruent triangles:

*Given:* $\angle 1 = \angle 4$
    E B is perpendicular to AC

*Prove:* ?????

The device of erasing what is to be proved helps build skills in inductive conjecturing as well as skills in deductive reasoning. Students begin to acquire the skills of anticipating and discovering for themselves the mathematics that we as teachers are often tempted to tell them. There is nothing duller for a geometry student, particularly a bright one, than to have the teacher announce every theorem and then prove it. It is far more interesting to have the theorems evolve inductively from class discussion. As in any inductive process many examples must be considered before a generalization can be formulated. For maximum interest, teachers should not take sides in arguments over student speculations. Rather we should solicit opinions, get all students involved, and encourage a proof or a counterexample (without indicating which is needed).

Coaxing conjectures out of students requires a game-like atmosphere. Indeed, geometry is like a game in which the students as detectives try to squeeze as much information as they can from postulates, definitions, and previous theorems. Sometimes the students' ideas come from experimentation with physical objects and drawings. For example, they can fold paper triangles so as to bisect the three angles. As they compare their folds with those of their classmates, someone inevitably surmises that in any triangle the angle bisectors meet in a point.

Students can be encouraged to make conjectures from drawings too. For example, ask students to draw an arbitrary quadrilateral and then join the midpoints of its sides in order. One student may speculate that a rectangle is formed only to have others quickly show their drawings in which this is not the case. When at last the students prove that the figure formed is a parallelogram, there remains the interesting question: What was so special about the first student's figure that caused a rectangle to be formed?

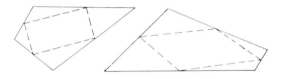

Another way to encourage students to make their own discoveries is to introduce coordinates sometime before studying parallelograms. Then when students plot the four vertices of a particular given parallelogram ABCD and observe that both diagonals have the same midpoint, some will wonder, or the teacher may ask, whether this will be true for other parallelograms. After observing that it is, some will want to know if this is true for all parallelograms. And is it ever true for non-parallelograms?

The point is that the use of coordinates to investigate properties of specific figures whose coordinates are given leads students to make generalizations. The proofs of these generalizations can be either with or without coordinates. By having both methods of proof shown, the theorem is reinforced and students sometimes see that one method is easier than another. Here are two specific examples:

*Easier with Coordinates:* The segment joining midpoints of two sides of a triangle is parallel to the third side and half as long.
*Easier without Coordinates:* The perpendicular bisectors of the sides of a triangle are concurrent.

Incidentally, another good reason for introducing coordinates early (even if your textbook does not) is to reinforce the students' algebra. If algebra skills are not kept alive, the student's next course will become more difficult because such courses usually draw more heavily on previous algebra than on previous geometry.

It can be stimulating to have the class record in an "official class text" the postulates, definitions, and theorems that evolve from their activities and discussions. Although many of the theorems will be standard ones that have been known for over two thousand years, the results will be new to the students. Their discovery is often exciting enough to warrant naming the theorem for the student discoverer. In my class last year, for example, the Balay-Siegal Theorem (which states that a quadrilateral is a parallelogram if its diagonals bisect each other) was named for the girl who conjectured the result and for the boy who proved it. Next year the same result will probably be named for someone else.

When students write their own text, they are more apt to learn two important lessons. First, the order in which theorems are given can vary. Neither Euclid nor their teacher has the only possible deductive sequence. Secondly, students realize that definitions are somewhat arbitrary and need not be handed down from on high. They learn that there are good definitions ("good" in the sense of mathematically useful) and bad ones.

Students also learn to live with the consequences of their definitions. For example, consider the following two definitions of a rhombus:

*Definition 1:* A rhombus is a quadrilateral with four equal sides.
*Definition 2:* A rhombus is a parallelogram with four equal sides.

If you wish to show that PQRS is a rhombus, definition 1 means less work for you. On the other hand, if ABCD is known to be a rhombus, definition 2 tells you more about the figure than definition 1. Usually students come to see that the best strategy here is to accept definition 1 and then immediately prove that a rhombus so defined is also a parallelogram. With practice in making definitions students come to see the usefulness of minimal definitions.

The possibility that different people may have different definitions or a different sequence of theorems is an important lesson. It is part of a larger lesson we should try to teach in all of our courses — namely, that mathematics is a human invention and a personal experience. These characteristics stand in marked contrast to many students' previous notions of mathematics as "right or wrong." So ingrained are these notions of rigidity that many people learn much mathematics by rote without thought. And so for many secondary students, the opportunity to invent some mathematics for themselves is a new experience.

We as teachers can foster this experience in several ways. We have already discussed the game-like atmosphere for geometry, the open-ended "What can *you* prove?" approach, the encouragement of experiments and drawings followed by inductive guesses, and the writing of a class text. Another fruitful technique is for the teacher to continually ask whether generalizations from one problem can be applied more broadly. Here are some examples:

*Example of a Theorem:* The perpendicular bisectors of the sides of a triangle meet in a point which is the center of the circumscribing circle.

*What are the generalizations of this theorem?*

(1) What other figures have the perpendicular bisectors of their sides concurrent? An arbitrary quadrilateral? A rectangle? A rhombus? A regular pentagon? Any prisms?

(2) What is the 3-dimensional analogue of this theorem? (The perpendicular bisecting planes of the sides of a triangular pyramid meet in a point which is the center of the circumscribing sphere.)

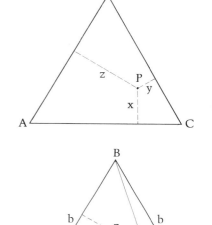

*Example of an Original Problem:* P is a point on or inside an equilateral triangle and x, y, and z are the perpendicular distances from P to the sides of the figure. What position of P makes the sum x + y + z least?

*Solution:* Students usually draw a large equilateral triangle, plot P in various locations, and discover that x + y + z seems to be the same no matter where P is. A proof of why this is so makes a challenging one-question homework assignment for a good class.

*A proof:*
Area $\triangle$ ABC = Area $\triangle$ PAC + Area $\triangle$ PCB + Area $\triangle$ PBA

$$\tfrac{1}{2}bh = \tfrac{1}{2}bx \qquad + \qquad \tfrac{1}{2}by \qquad + \qquad \tfrac{1}{2}bz$$

Thus, h = x + y + z

*What are the generalizations of this problem?*

(1) Equilateral triangles can be generalized to regular polygons.

(2) There is a 3-dimensional version of the problem in which the areas of the triangles mentioned in the proof above are replaced by volumes of pyramids.

This last generalization may be too much for all but your very best students, but the general principle remains: encourage your students to determine whether a given result is a special case of a more general result.

Also get your students to question what happens when the conditions of a problem are altered. For example, it should become almost standard procedure to think about the converse of any statement proved as a theorem. It is also useful to raise the question of the inverse of a theorem. Here are some questions involving inverses.

*Theorem:* In triangle ABC, if a = b, then ∠A = ∠B.
*Questions:* What can you say about ∠A and ∠B if a>b? if a<b?
*Theorem:* If triangle ABC has ∠C = 90°, then $c^2 = a^2 + b^2$.
*Question:* What is the relationship between a, b, and c, if ∠C is acute or obtuse?

It would be a mistake to assume that the discover-it-yourself approach to mathematics works for all students. Syllabus demands are such that some classes do not have the time needed to use this technique for sustained periods of time. Even for those classes that do have the time, some students find it easier to be told what to learn and then to memorize it. This approach can be a quick way to acquire facts, but the point of this essay is that there is much more to mathematics than the specific theorems and formulas learned. We should try to expose our students to the personal, inventive aspect of learning mathematics. It can be argued that for most students the process of arriving at formulas and theorems through experimenting, guessing and deduction is at least as important as the formulas and theorems themselves. This process can be used throughout life in other disciplines even when specific mathematical facts are not needed.

# IV

## "... a stimulating pace"

# MODERN LANGUAGES

Janet E. Kehl

As THE FIVE-MINUTE BELL rings, students pour in for the first day of classes, some boisterous, loquacious, gregarious, others hesitant, silent, reserved. Whatever the mixture, tension mounts with the arrival of each newcomer. Students shift nervously in their seats while the teacher shuffles needlessly through materials. As all falls quiet, fourteen expectant faces turn toward the teacher. With equal curiosity, the teacher scans this chorus of new faces, looking for the individual behind each bright set of eyes and for some hint of the identity of the group. How will these different talents and personalities blend? Will this class be serious, playful, stubborn, willing? Will these separate voices find a new common language in an unfamiliar tongue?

If, in the last moment of silence before the class begins, the teacher is as anxious as the students, it is because the teacher has so little time to bring this group of individuals together and to lead them toward a new language. Teachers know that they have but a few weeks to discover the invisible fifteenth student called the class and to find a *modus vivendi* for this unique combination of abilities and personalities. They know that if each individual is to learn, the teacher must find the tone, the materials, and the methods that best suit that fifteenth student.

From the first word of the class, the most immediate and most difficult task of the teacher is to set a tone that will combat the spectre that haunts every foreign language classroom, inhibition. The inhibited student will never achieve a spontaneous use of the language, nor will he ever enjoy the liberation of a new mode of expression. In a class of able adolescents, that inhibition may have many sources: it may be fear of competition; it may be a feeling of insecurity that comes when a person is reduced to the communicative level of a three-year-old; it may be timidity before one's peers or a particular individual in the class. It is thus the responsibility of the teacher first and foremost to establish an atmosphere that fosters cooperation, confidence, and communication.

There is no better way to encourage such an atmosphere than to get students to talk, to each other and to the teacher. Often, a few minutes of conversation while waiting for class to begin will open shy mouths or set the tone for the hour. That conversation may be in French and so provide a natural and relaxed transition into the lesson, or it may be in English, giving the students a chance to be themselves in a way that the prohibition of English during class prevents. In class, there are countless ways to use the material to make students talk to each other. With new vocabulary words, have them ask one another serious or amusing questions. With interrogative pronouns make them interview each other. When reading *Le Petit Prince*, let each student "tame" a classmate. To ensure that the students also talk individually to the teacher, establish the rule that any student who lapses into English during the lesson must have a five or ten minute tête-à-tête in French with the teacher out of class.

Much more subtle is the attitude of the teacher toward each individual and toward the group. Students are quick to sense preferences, dislikes, and injustices. If teachers are to develop a healthy sense of community, they must make sure that individual students sense their own values within the group. Teachers must also be careful how they convey any displeasure or frustration. Bright adolescents are sometimes too apt to assume their own failures and to withdraw or lash out defensively. Because they are, for the most part, still so unsure of themselves, they also need to be told both as individuals and as a group when they have done something well. Teachers working with able students must not become so inured to quick answers and spirited classes that they fail to recognize how well a student or a class may have handled difficult material.

As fundamental as the ambiance is the choice of materials. In choosing the right materials for able students the teacher must not forget the students' need to be challenged. Since talented students demand that their reason, imagination, and judgment be engaged as well as their memory, teachers must walk a tight rope. They must not choose works that are so far beyond the ability of the students that frustration impedes learning. But neither should the teacher choose selections that are too puerile for the intellectual and emotional sophistication of maturing teenagers. Never underestimate the tenacity of the student who is intellectually challenged.

At the introductory levels, able students, particularly upperclassmen, are impatient with materials that are too simpleminded. Texts that present too specialized or juvenile a vocabulary alienate them. Why dally in the barnyard with the farmer and his wife when the students will learn more with their French counterparts at the café? Students able and accustomed to assimilating considerable amounts of information are equally frustrated by texts that spread the explanation of a grammatical point through too many chapters; they want to learn more than one variation on a theme at a time and feel cheated if the text always spares them the exception to the rule. Similarly, too many simplistic exercises that require repetition, obvious substitutions and combinations, or simple recall bore them. To hold their attention, they need exercises that involve choice, complex structural changes, and creativity.

Students at these levels are also quick to reject too much artificiality. The contrived conversations and inane stories of many elementary texts may well lessen student enthusiasm for the language and the culture. Colloquial dialogues and culturally authentic situations are more likely to capture their interests. Informative paragraphs about the culture should also be included to increase the students' awareness of the style of life behind the language. Finally, the teacher, even at this level, should introduce some simple literature so that the students are exposed to the living language.

At the intermediate level, where students are beginning to study more literature than grammar, the major difficulty in the choice of materials is the discrepancy between the student's maturity and fluency in the foreign language. A student who in his English class is reading Shakespeare, Dostoevski, and Joyce has little interest in the adventure stories and mysteries that ninth and tenth graders might yet enjoy. Intellectually, the student is ready to conceptualize and to think critically, but lexically, he is limited in his ability to read and to articulate his ideas.

To keep pace with the student's maturing mind and sustain his interest the teacher must use materials that require analysis and stimulate debate. There are ways to make a difficult text manageable. Speed up the reading by handing out vocabulary lists that save the student the tedium and discontinuity of using the dictionary too frequently and by providing questions that guide the student through the text. Discussions in class will flow more smoothly if students have had a chance to formulate ideas in answer to these questions. The discussion may be even better if the students themselves bring in questions or if they begin class by writing a brief answer to a question that will be discussed during the rest of the class.

At the advanced levels, the problem reverses. The text that is appropriate linguistically may be stylistically or culturally beyond even the bright student. Racine, for example, will not move most American adolescents. The teacher must therefore be especially careful at this level not to confuse the students' natural ability with the literary and cultural sophistication necessary to understand and appreciate many works. If Racine is to be assigned, be prepared to supplement the text with explanations of 17th-century values and literary conventions.

In deciding which methods to use teachers must consider the needs and capacities of their students as much as the demands of the subject matter. In teaching able and motivated teenagers, teachers should depend not so much on one particular method as on a combination of techniques that serve the students' need for a stimulating pace, for variety, and for a balance between highly structured and creative activities. Students also need opportunities to play in the language. Above all, it is the student, not the teacher, who should take the dominant role in the class.

Good serious students have little patience with a sluggish pace — especially at the lower levels. Impatient with too much repetition, they demand that new material be introduced at a rate that may at times exceed the ability to assimilate it. During the progress of a course teachers must ensure assimilation with adequate review, but must also move ahead quickly enough to sustain the students' sense of accomplishment. In each class the pace must be brisk enough to keep students alert and yet not so fast that it intimidates or discourages beginners. To regulate the pace teachers must evaluate each activity: the length of the question, the amount of reaction time, the length of the response, and the duration of the entire exercise. A two-minute drill requiring one-word responses obviously imposes a faster pace than an eight-word pattern drill or a series of questions. Armed with information about their drills, teachers can change the tempo to suit their purposes. To begin a low-level class *largo*, for example, is a mistake when every mouth can be set in motion *allegro vivace* with a rapid-fire short answer exercise. Teachers may then use the momentum to hold the students' attention through a more complicated activity or the presentation of new material. Like composers, teachers modulate the tempo from intensity in certain exercises to relaxation in others.

Teachers must also not forget how much their own participation and presence affect the pace of a class. They must know when to add or remove their own voices from an exercise, whether to respond quickly or slowly to a student response or question. Even teachers' movements are important; gestures, eye contact, posture, movement around the classroom may all accelerate or moderate the pace. At the low levels in particular, teachers should never underestimate how much their energy and vivacity influence the students.

To find and maintain an appropriate pace at the upper levels is much more difficult. Students and teacher alike become so used to frequent changes of tempo, to immediate responses, and to a certain intensity that both must learn to adapt to the slower pace required by materials that demand reflection and much more complex articulation of ideas. Furthermore, students who are straining in a discussion to understand the language as well as the ideas of classmates often have difficulty sustaining that discussion for an entire class. The teacher's problem at these levels, then, is how to slow down enough to allow for thoughtful discussion but not so much as to exhaust the student's power of concentration. With students coming from the brisk pace of the first two years, teachers cannot slow down immediately, but must gradually wean them from the torrent of words and the flurry of activities to which they have been accustomed. They must allow for and sometimes even impose silences until the students overcome the impulse to fill every silence immediately without thinking. They must limit discussions and change activities within each lesson until the students are sufficiently familiar with the language of a work or topic to express themselves and comprehend each other readily, and until they are involved enough in the work or topic to carry on a prolonged discussion.

Variety and novelty are just as important as an invigorating pace. Repeating the same activity is ineffective at any level — whether within the same class or day after day. A student who learns from one pattern drill is not likely to absorb much from three in a row requiring the same mental process even though the structure is changed in each. Students who at first eagerly answer questions about a reading selection often hold back after too many days of the same procedure. Language learning requires repetition of both material and class activities, but teachers can alleviate the tedium if they use ingenuity as well as careful planning.

Fortunately the wide range of skills to be learned offers plenty of opportunity for variety. Teachers must cover the four linguistic skills of listening, speaking, reading, and writing, at the lower levels every day and at the upper levels every week. They must also be sure to include a variety of cognitive skills — mimicry, recall, recognition, association, discrimination, reconstruction, and innovation — within each lesson and a variety of procedures to exercise these skills within a series of lessons. Tedium may also be relieved if teachers deviate occasionally from the academic routine. Novelty energizes, and an unexpected film, record or tape, song, game, or excursion to the local pâtisserie may revitalize students for several weeks.

Whatever the activities, they must be carefully balanced between those that are highly structured and the less structured creative ones if the student is to learn to speak and write the language accurately and naturally. Students are not speaking the language if the words that they spout lack the proper grammar and syntax, nor if their words, for all their accuracy, are not their own but merely responses unrelated to a context that lends them meaning. Students need highly structured exercises to learn the skeleton of the language and creative ones to transform recitation into communication. Because bright students derive satisfaction from seeing and applying structure, they learn readily from pattern drills, verb synopses, or translations, but they also need the opportunity to formulate sentences of their own, to play with the structures they have learned, and to respond spontaneously. If language, as Karl Diller defines it, is "rule-governed creativity," then a combination of structured and creative oral and written activities is needed to respond to the needs of the bright student for structure and innovation and to the demands of the subject matter.[1]

In moving from schoolroom language to genuine language students need to progress from highly structured exercises to those with a minimum of structure. If, for example, students are learning the use of the subjunctive after certain conjunctions, they need to begin with drills that combine two given clauses or that require substitution either of the conjunction or verb. Next they are asked to complete sentences with their own subordinate clauses given a conjunction and a subject. Finally they create entire sentences of their own, given only the conjunction or given a word or picture as cue and choosing their own conjunctions. At the lower and intermediate levels, the teacher may repeat this progression with every new grammatical point or reading selection as well as use it as a guideline for the entire course, so that by the end of each semester, students are using the material as spontaneously as possible. In advanced courses, where students respond naturally at a more creative level, a similar progression from directive to less directive questions or activities helps the development of interpretive and writing skills.

Closely related to the need for structured and creative activity is the need for play, for play is, in effect, also "rule-governed creativity." In *Homo Ludens: A Study of the Play-Element in Culture*, Johan Huizinga asserts that "next to *Homo Faber*, and perhaps on the same level as *Homo Sapiens*, *Homo Ludens*, Man the Player, deserves a place in our nomenclature."[2] The anthropologist may not agree with Huizinga's characterization of man, but anyone who has taught adolescents would hardly contest that they play more often than they build or think. So why not exploit that love of play in the language classroom?

1. Karl C. Diller, "Linguistic Theories of Language Acquisition," in *Teaching a Living Language* (New York, Harper & Row, 1970), p. 13

2. Johan Huizinga, *Homo Ludens: A Study of the Play-Element in Culture* (Boston, Beacon Press, 1980), p. ix.

Huizinga describes play as

> a free activity standing quite consciously outside "ordinary" life as being "not serious," but at the same time absorbing the player intensely and utterly. It is an activity connected with no material interest, and no profit can be gained by it. It proceeds within its own proper boundaries of time and space according to fixed rules and in an orderly manner. It promotes the formation of social groupings. . . . [3]

As such, play serves the needs of the adolescent, of the language learner, and of the class as a group. Unlike many classroom activities, play involves "intensely and utterly" not only the mind but also the emotions so that the adolescent brings a more complete, more integrated, and more committed self to the language experience. Play also demands the pure, spontaneous use of the language to meet goals that are more basic than the usually self-conscious goal of learning the language.

As in the case of role-playing, play offers the opportunity to replace lifeless mimicry with Aristotelian mimesis. Since play is "connected with no material interest" but is a pleasure in and of itself, it is so gratifying and enjoyable that it encourages and motivates the student. While play is serving the individual it is also, as Huizinga notes, helping a set of individuals to function as a group: students who have supported and entertained each other while playing will then work better together and learn more from each other.

Students and the teacher can play in a foreign language in many ways. On the simplest level, they play with words or grammatical structures. They play word games such as anagrams, Ghost, Scrabble, Boggle, or charades. They interview celebrities dead or alive or fictitious characters. They write riddles. At a more complex and creative level, they role-play, either in small groups, where each individual plays a role, or as a class, where a set of three or four students assumes one role. They play out or modify a scene from the reading or add scenes of their own invention. They produce skits based on a set of vocabulary words from the day's lesson or based on a given situation or an object pulled blindly from a paper bag. They im-

---

3. *Ibid.*, p. 13.

provise a dialogue between real or imaginary characters. The possibilities are endless.

In games or any classroom activity the teacher must ensure that the student assumes an active role. Although students learn by listening and reading, they learn more by speaking and writing, in effect, by "doing" in the foreign language. The teacher must first make sure that this "doing" is activity that engages the mind and emotions of the students, not just time-consuming mechanical performing. The student must also be active at a level commensurate with his ability and proficiency.

In order to expand the role of the student in the class, teachers must minimize their own. Above all, they must avoid doing for students what students alone or with the help of classmates can do for themselves. Instead of explaining, teachers should try to lead students to discover the grammatical structure or idea for themselves. Rather than correct careless errors, teachers should make the students correct them. Rather than present themselves as the sole source of drills, questions, corrections, and answers, they must demand that students fulfill those functions for each other. They must wean the students away from the teacher by training them to learn independently from the material and from each other. They must prepare students for that day when there will be no teacher.

Training students to do as much as possible for themselves requires not less work and preparation on the part of the teacher but more. The teacher should have no illusions about how much time it takes to find and adapt materials and methods for each new group of students. To lead each class from structured to innovative use of the language, to devise activities that progressively minimize the participation of the teacher, to supplement texts and exercises require much thought and planning. No textbook or literary work will by itself provide the means of liberating a student or a class. Only the teacher who takes the time to know the students and to use materials creatively in response to each class's needs and interests can provide the structure. And only the teacher who finds the time to keep abreast of new materials and methods will have the flexibility to do so.

Teachers must also find the time, if they are to keep the language alive in the classroom, to renew their own contacts with the foreign culture, for every language reflects the values and customs of a nation, of a place. To omit such cultural considerations from the language classroom is to limit the student's understanding of the language and to deprive him of the benefit of exposure to a different lifestyle. To convey the vitality of the language and the culture, teachers must feel it themselves. They must leave the classroom behind to immerse themselves regularly in the culture. For the French teacher, no book, film, or course can substitute for Paris or Québec.

Teaching a foreign language is like directing a chorus. From varying talents and voices teachers must draw forth accurate, expressive and gratifying sound. From each student they must elicit the best performance and from the group the most harmonious blend of voices. To each rehearsal they must bring a score that is appropriate to the ability, maturity, and interest of the singers and that the teachers, because of their own studies, travels and experiences, understand and appreciate. During each rehearsal of that score, they must keep the tempo, vary the dynamics and allow for repetition and improvisation. For inexperienced singers teachers may often sing a part, with more advanced ones they may sometimes sing along, but ultimately, they must bring the chorus to sing without accompaniment. If the teacher and the class have succeeded at all, they will feel, in the moment's silence that precedes the downbeat of the last class, not the tension of the first day, but a sense of exhilaration.

# MUSIC

A. Irving Forbes

THE QUESTION of identifying and dealing with talent looms persistently before all of us who teach music. It is an intensely personal problem because while we are seeking to foster talent in others, we continually wonder whether we are sufficiently talented ourselves. We know that to do our job well we must be both musician and teacher; we cannot be one without being the other. We also know that we need personal qualities of patience, understanding and kindness, since some of our work is with those who are inexperienced musically. Their intellects are active, their minds are open and talent may be there, but they lack musical training.

Musicianship consists of many elements. Physically, one must have ears that are trained to discriminate fine variations in pitch, tone, rhythm and volume. Fingers, tongue and/or arms must be coordinated to move at high and steady speeds. Eyes must be trained to grasp a large part of a page while reading scores. On the intellectual side, the memory must be enlarged to retain a long string of notes, measures and phrases just as a storyteller would recall a complex series of events. Finally, experience, imagination and wit must be blended to create a being who is original, sensitive and what we vaguely call artistic. We seek these skills in ourselves and in others.

In applied music one of the first tasks of the music teacher is to identify performers with talent. As we listen to students perform, we evaluate their work. We observe whether they simply rattle through a piece with measured perfection, or whether they play with some concept of where the piece is going. We look for a small measure of the students' individuality and artistry in their interpretation. More specifically, we watch for a sense of phrasing, a feeling for the movement of notes to a climax with a subsequent relaxation of tension. We observe whether there is articulation within a phrase which points up moments of stress and emphasis. Once we have identified especially talented performers, we do all we can to encourage them to develop their skills as far as possible.

Our goals with intermediate performers are different. With these students we are concerned that they achieve as much facility on their chosen instruments as possible, since this period in their lives is the one when the greatest strides in physical speed and accurate coordination can be made. We rarely encourage students to consider music as a profession, but we would like them to reach their potential so that they are equipped to take a seat in a good college or community orchestra, or to be a leader rather than a follower in a fine choral group.

In teaching courses on music on the secondary level, we seek to broaden the horizons of beginners so that they may become more enlightened members of the audience world. To do so we acquaint beginners with the variety of musical forms from early plainsong through expanded sonata form. The study of musical form naturally leads to a definition of the major periods in history. Where possible, parallels are drawn with the corresponding periods in art, architecture and literature. As more musical examples are heard, the students become aware of the sound of specific composers. They learn to identify them by the shape of their melodies, the thickness of their harmonies, the complexity of their counterpoint and by the transparency or massiveness of their orchestration. To comprehend orchestration students have to be taught — through demonstrations — to recognize the timbre of all orchestral instruments.

Most formal courses in music at the secondary level are either Music Appreciation or Harmony. Music Appreciation is usually chosen by those with little experience in musicmaking. If asked at the beginning of the course what they most want to get out of it, most students reply that they want to know how music is put together. They are curious about form and the tools of the composer's trade, about the way in which movements of a symphony relate to one another, about whether the composer uses instruments singly or in combination. They ask how the composer develops and expands tiny motifs into themes and themes into phrases, how interest is sustained between climaxes, and what is the composer's grand psychological plan. Although teachers try to satisfy this curiosity, it is not always possible to answer every question in one course.

Music Appreciation usually begins with basic theory, with the class singing major and minor scales, triads and all the intervals. It is also a good idea to sing "tah, tah, tahs" in many rhythmic patterns and in various meters while conducting. Student reaction is often hilarious. If football players complain about the difficulty of singing and conducting simultaneously, I tell them that if they have enough coordination to complete a forward pass or to tackle an opponent, they have enough for music.

When symphonies are being studied, the main themes are written on the board, and the class is expected to sing, moan or groan on pitch all of the themes — and to continue singing these themes on the way to their next class. Dvořák's *New World Symphony* has thirteen singable themes, many of which can be superimposed upon each other. Dvořák intended it that way. Trying to sing these themes in class can be both rewarding and riotous.

In Music Appreciation, or in any other music course, learning by doing has much more appeal than learning by being told. Often, for expediency, we indulge in the latter, but we all know that learning sticks longer when achieved by the former. Certainly, intellectualizing about the emotional effect of a diminished chord means far less to the music student than singing the theme to "Dragnet" (which begins with a broken diminished chord). The more we can associate the intervals found in the major and minor scales with the same intervals that occur in a fragment of a familiar tune, the more lasting will be this basic musical concept. Students soon volunteer their own examples of a major seventh interval, for instance. The same is true of rhythmic patterns. After the class has sung a fragment of rhythm written on the board, the students can then discover the same rhythm in any number of pieces of their acquaintance.

Courses in harmony, ordinarily offered to students who have had some previous musical training, are best divided according to ability. To determine who should be in the advanced section, ask all candidates to write out the first six measures of "America," melody only. Then test the students on recognition of intervals and rhythmic patterns. Finally, have each person play four measures of a simple hymn, if possible in four-part harmony, and, failing all else, with one finger on the soprano part. The correlation among the results of these trials is usually good.

In many ways the study of harmony is similar to the study of the grammar of a foreign language. Both can be tedious but need not be. In each case the teacher has to insist on a thorough knowledge of many rules as well as their correct application in a variety of situations. A student can become frustrated when impatient to get ahead on an intellectual plane while lacking command of technicalities. In French or music it is not easy to teach good usage, appropriateness and variety while maintaining unity, for the meaning of these terms is rather nebulous to the young student.

As soon as fluency is gained, students harmonize their own original melodies. On some creative projects it is exciting to give the students complete freedom, enough rope to see how skillfully they can slip through the noose. Do they follow the rules of the textbook, or do they bend the rules to achieve an original effect? Do they wallow around and say nothing, or do they come up with something really worth playing? Most frustrating to the teacher are students who write something outrageous, and who, after mild criticism, insist they like it that way. Teachers do not want to stand in the way of potentially creative talent; yet we have to tell stubborn students that their compositions are so far removed from the common practice of other composers that they might not sell very well in their present form.

No one agrees on how to judge free creations or what criteria may be used for something as abstract as music. The task can only be compared with evaluating an abstract painting. Does the piece make any sense? Is it satisfying in some way? Does it bear repeated hearing or viewing? When teachers feel powerless to criticize intelligently, they can ask each class member to write out criticisms anonymously and turn the paragraphs over to the composer. These critiques are usually candid and kind and almost always helpful to the recipient.

An ideal music program in a large school should also include the opportunity for private lessons as well as an orchestra, a glee club and a stage band. Regular curricular offerings might also include a choir and wind and string instrumental ensembles, which are chosen after careful auditioning. Course credit should be given for private lessons or for participation in the choir or the ensembles because the work is academically worthwhile and because preparation for these courses is equal to that in comparable academic courses. The most talented and serious students could carry one-fourth of their workload in applied music and receive full academic credit for practicing eight or more hours a week and giving a recital at the end of the course. The stage band encourages jazz musicians to try their hand at forming smaller combos, where improvisation is very much in order. Though some of the results are monotonous and loud enough to threaten ear damage, a few combos develop a style which is musically interesting.

The music department of a large school should present a series of concerts throughout the year. Many of these will consist of students singly or in ensembles, others will be presented by faculty and guest artists. Taping the concerts provides the performers with a chance to evaluate their own playing and sometimes reinforces the comments of the teacher. A concerto competition adds a great deal to each year. After the best contestants are selected, they can be honored by having their concertos presented in a concert accompanied by the orchestra. This is particularly rewarding to the accomplished pianists, who otherwise would never have this exciting ensemble experience.

The teachers who run these programs and give courses and lessons should also be active performers because performing makes them better teachers. It makes them more sympathetic than otherwise to the technical problems facing their students. It also enables them to bring their colleagues to the school for ensemble work and for faculty recitals. Classroom music teachers, therefore, have a double professional obligation: they must maintain not only their teaching skills but also their ability to perform. They must remain familiar with the literature of the instrument they are teaching and they must maintain their association with other professionals, who will keep them musically alert. And their own playing should provide good examples for their pupils. It is unfortunate when music teachers succumb to the teaching load and let their instrumental technique slide.

Sometimes students are surprised to learn that a teacher is

taking a summer course after having taught for many years. Performers must perform and teachers must get new ideas, for the teacher-performer who can no longer learn should be buried alive, or at least retire early. The exciting and engrossing activity of effective teaching should keep music teachers young and very much alive well into their retirement. In conjunction with teaching, the joy and challenge of musicmaking on some level should continue as long as physically possible. This combination should serve as an inspiration and as an example for students.

# CLASSICS

David D. Coffin

IF THE IDEAL EDUCATION, to adapt an old saying to the classics, is Aristotle at one end of a log and Alexander at the other, it becomes necessary, in order to apply this maxim, to identify Aristotles and Alexanders and to say something about logs. It is significant that there is nothing in the saying about books, and little will be said here on that subject, but it seems wise to add a few conjectures about what Aristotle might be saying to Alexander and how he might say it.

THE TEACHER

In a field as varied and as technical as classics, professional training is of paramount importance. Talented students who choose a difficult course are often full of enthusiasm and want to move ahead rapidly. If the teacher is giving himself on-the-job training, is having a hard time keeping up with the class, or is answering questions with uncertainty, students are aware of it, and their enthusiasm is blunted. (I have noticed that if I have only a general knowledge of the answer to a student's question, my reply is at least three times too long, and no one is listening at the end. "I'll look that up" is a response that must be used sparingly, especially since by the time the answer has been produced, it is often of little interest any longer. And the time-worn evasion, "Why don't you look it up, Bob, and report to the class tomorrow," quickly teaches Bob not to ask interesting questions.) A teacher with a knowledge of the history of a language, not just the language itself, can often, especially in Greek, give a general concept which will explain a series of difficulties to students talented enough to be interested in patterns rather than memorizing isolated forms. Moreover, for students able to grasp the whole picture it helps if the classics teacher is not only a linguist and littérateur, but a bit of an archeologist, historian, and sociologist, and can also bring to class artifacts that help enliven the words of the text.

Here is where the question of training comes in. An undergraduate major and graduate school work in the field of classics are helpful in shaping curriculum because they give a general view of the field and show which writings are interesting or important and how difficult they are. Such training is especially useful in day-to-day work because it shows where to go for more information. A graduate course in linguistics is also of great practical value. Teacher training and practice teaching are far less valuable than solid academic training.

But whatever the training, what the teacher does in daily and long-term preparation is the most crucial part of good teaching . In classics there is no such thing as being too familiar with the daily reading lesson. Particularly if the students are bright, the teacher needs to have read the assigned work and notes as recently as they have in order to be able to answer their often complicated questions promptly and to maintain the pace so essential for such students. It slows down a class if teachers discuss points already explained in the notes.

Of equal importance is the longer-term preparation of reading periodicals and books in the field as well as keeping an eye out for newspaper articles, pictures, and even cartoons that relate to the classics. (I once took away the menu of the Boston Museum of Fine Arts Restaurant because it had on it a picture of a coin both sides of which related to a poem of Catullus.) Teachers will find interesting ideas and information in almost every issue of the *American Journal of Philology, Classical Journal, Classical Review, Classical Philology, Classical World, Greece & Rome, Transactions of the American Philological Association,* and *Vergilius.* Some of these such as the *Classical Journal* have articles on teaching, and most have literary and historical articles that offer something to take into class. The magazines contain lists of new books and reviews of books, on the basis of which the teacher can make suggestions for the school library. *Classical World* contains useful bibliographies of classical authors and an annual list of textbooks in print and audiovisual materials available.

THE STUDENT

Because we think so frequently of aptitude in terms of verbal

(English, history) and quantitative (mathematics, science), it is important in discussing language study to remember that linguistic, like musical or artistic, aptitude can be something distinct from verbal or mathematical talent. When talented students are brought together, many of them are going to be un-talented in one or more fields of study.

In the classical languages, where the class generally must proceed at a uniform pace, remarkable things can be accomplished if those who prove in the first year to be linguistically gifted are sectioned separately from the rest. Some flexibility in sectioning must exist, however, for the purely mathematically talented can often keep up with the linguists in the first year or so, while those linguists who have literary skills as well have the advantage in the more advanced courses.

Furthermore, among the linguistically talented there appear to be two skills. Any method of teaching should take into account students who have either. Those who have both are few indeed; they are the stars of any classical language course. One of these skills is largely intuitive; it seems to be related to the skill of those who in modern languages are said to have a "good ear," though in the classics the skill does not necessarily involve aural aptitude. It is the ability to grasp the meaning of a passage of Latin or Greek by knowing or looking up the meaning of the words without more than subconscious awareness of such grammatical items as tense, mood, and case. Owing to the inflected nature of the classical languages, the user of this skill often makes small errors and is sometimes completely wrong in his interpretation of a passage. Early in the course he also may have difficulty learning out-of-context material such as verb forms. He does, however, read more rapidly than other students and usually with better general comprehension.

The other skill is that of the student who can learn easily and remember accurately the endings that indicate tense, mood, and case and use them to deduce the meaning of the passage as he works through it more slowly. This student is often more accurate than the faster reader, but in his interest to explain each ending can lose the forest for the trees. He must be encouraged to read less analytically and with more regard for sense, just as his opposite number must be persuaded to develop an eye for detail. The two types can, however, coexist in a class and they learn from each other's strengths. Eventually a combination of skills must be achieved if a student is to be first-rate linguistically in the classics and build the strongest basis for literary skills.

## THE CLASS

As already mentioned, linguistically talented students can move at a pace that maintains their interest and accomplish a great deal more if they are sectioned separately from others. The opposing argument, that the presence of talented students in a class of mixed ability helps the less able students, may be a prevailing consideration in some other subjects, but in languages—and particularly in the early years—the differences in students' speed in assimilating new material and in the amount of practice needed in class are so great that ungraded sections deprive talented students and encourage mediocrity. Furthermore, there is in "fast" sections the "Hawthorne effect" — the individual's sometimes subconscious increase in effort when he knows that he is part of a select group. In many cases this effect exists automatically in Latin and Greek courses; sectioning increases it. Good students learn from each other in the daily interchange in class and sometimes can keep each other from becoming arrogant or overconfident. The inevitable sense of competition can be beneficial and can reduce cliquishness, which is a problem in a field as small as classics, where the able students are repeatedly in the same sections.

Size of class is an important consideration in language work. Although the class must be large enough to provide productive interchange, there is the danger in a world of limited budgets that the class will be too large to allow each student the opportunity for more than token practice at each meeting. What is more, above the elementary level the abler students have more to contribute to class discussion and should have time to express their opinions or to react to those of others. Ideally the number of students should be small enough to allow an informal arrangement of the class, such as around a seminar table.

## METHOD AND MATTER

Recent years have seen a multiplication of methods for introducing a student to Latin and Greek. New texts for the traditional method (deductive by paradigms and grammatical rules) continue to appear. There is also a wide variety of texts for Latin by reading which are more inductive than deductive: by the direct method (reading, but with no English used), by the structural method (nouns by case, verbs by person in order of frequency in Latin), by computer, by programmed text (in the manner of a teaching machine), and by transformational grammar (giving synonymous phrases in Latin). These methods, which overlap, are more suited to the student with intuitive linguistic skill, while the traditional method is easier for the student with the more analytical mind. In an experiment at Exeter a few years ago teaching Latin in a slightly modified version of the direct method, the truly able linguist appeared to learn as well as by the traditional method. The experiment showed, however, that for the other students, including a good percentage who would normally be classified as "talented," the direct method needed to be supported by a traditional workbook giving grammar and vocabulary. The most recent textbook for ancient Greek consists of two volumes: a reader and a separate book containing grammar, vocabulary, and exercises.

By the same token the traditional method is most effective in preparing students to read Latin or Greek when it is accompanied by a good deal of reading. The teacher should remember that the principal objective is for the student to learn to read the classical languages unadapted, although hearing, speaking, and writing the languages may be helpful in fulfilling that aim. A good method is to ask students to read Latin aloud before translating it in order to get them in the habit of approaching it as Latin; in addition, the teacher can tell by how well they read in class whether they are approaching it in this way in their homework. Talented students will reach the point where they frequently do not have to translate after reading a Latin sentence in Latin. The traditional method also serves the secondary purpose of giving the student an accurate sense of sentence structure and of the use of words, which carries over into speech and writing in any language. To this end a modest amount of converting English to Latin is helpful.

Whatever the method used for learning the basic structures of a classical language, a class of talented students can accomplish this task within an academic year. By the end of the year they can be reading Latin (or Greek) that is unadapted or only slightly simplified. Even good students, though, need a review of the first year after a summer's vacation, but the review can go hand-in-hand with reading one of the easier prose writers such as Caesar or Nepos in Latin. Caesar has been vilified in recent years by those compelled in their youth to spend a year reading *The Gallic War*, but a good text of Nepos is hard to come by, and some reading at Caesar's level of difficulty is needed to make the transition from "made" or adapted Latin to works of literary merit. Caesar can be interesting if the class reads only the highlights. It is remarkable how little Caesar needs to be read by good students before they are ready for something more difficult. In special sections at the beginning of the second year, two months is enough. Because this reading is less important than what will follow, and therefore less discussable, part of the time in class can be spent working on the formation of Latin words (prefixes and suffixes) and its relation to the formation of English words. The aim is to improve both Latin and English vocabulary.

Up to this point the students have principally been acquiring linguistic skills through reading, question-and-answer exercises and sometimes writing on the board. But after Caesar they begin to deal with style and content and hold discussions in class. They are expected to acquire a knowledge of figures of speech and other stylistic devices and to be able to show how these bring out or embellish the author's meaning. The organization of material is also discussed, for structure is an excellent way by which to understand and remember a work. Oratory is a logical style to begin with because it uses devices and organization more noticeably than other prose genres and serves as a stepping-stone to poetry. If oratory, then Cicero; and if Cicero, then the political, social, and cultural background of his works comes into discussion. Able students can study Cicero in exactly the same depth that the Advanced Placement Program expects of students of Virgil, Catullus, and Horace. To make this possible books containing background information on the author and his times, books on and scholarly editions of the work, and general reference material (such as classical dictionaries and handbooks) should be readily accessible in the school library or a reading room. These books can be used for outside reading assignments, for ready reference for those with questions, and for the assistance of those who want to do a particularly good job on the day's work. They also make it possible at the literature levels for able students to teach a substantial portion of a class. The aim is to interest them in the scholarly resources available and to show them how good a job they can do on an assignment if they wish to. Usually after teaching they have more to contribute in class and what they say is more relevant to the literary qualities of the work.

From the level of Cicero on the teacher should begin to give tests that include essay questions and that put emphasis on style, structure, content, and background. Sight translation is valuable at all levels. Students are asked to put into good English a previously unseen passage of Latin with familiar words and constructions. With good students it is an excellent guide to what progress they are making in reading Latin as well as an exercise in converting Latin to idiomatic English. Comprehension tests (an unseen passage not to be translated, but with questions to answer about its meaning) do not always work well with talented students. Often the test will not discriminate because either they will all get a general idea of the sense and deduce the rest with the help of the questions, or if the passage is made more difficult, many will not grasp it at all.

Cicero can be an enlightening and even exciting experience, but since a good pace must be maintained, a few months is enough for talented students. After doing a little Ovid to introduce the hexameter, good students can start the Advanced Placement Virgil course midway through the second year. At first, owing to the novelty of poetic expression, the density of Virgil's style, and the unfamiliarity of classical metrics, the students move slowly, reading aloud a great deal and translating every word. Some memorization is required, to build a feeling for the rhythm and to stress important passages. Eventually translation problems can be taken care of with a question period at the beginning of the class, and more time can be left for discussion of style and content and for introducing the topic of symbolism, to which most good students respond eagerly. There should also be a limited amount of outside reading. By the end of the second year the best students have had some Cicero and some Virgil and have fulfilled most schools' concept of a language requirement.

Most, however, are likely to continue and complete the Advanced Placement Virgil course in the third fall followed by the Advanced Placement Lyric Poetry course (Catullus and Horace) by the end of the third year. The short lyric poems call for a different approach from that of the long epic, and critiques of poems, dealing with structure, style, and imagery, are assigned as short papers outside of class and written in class.

Thus bright students can be introduced in three years to a broad array of skills and to as varied a selection of reading as they might have in four and a half years at a traditional pace. Although the primary purpose of the speed is to create challenge and interest for the talented, an additional benefit is obtained in making more academic time available, time which can be used for advanced study in Latin, for a complementary course in Greek, or for broadening into an entirely different field.

In Greek, because virtually all the students are talented, the program is similarly accelerated. The students read unadapted easy prose (Xenophon) by the end of the first year. In the second year, after a little more easy prose and a review of fundamentals, the first semester is spent on Plato, and the second on Homer. Plato affords some splendid reading with opportunities for learning in the fields of both literary prose and philosophy; while Homer provides easy reading in poetry along with a whole range of new skills to be learned—in metrics, linguistics, and literary criticism. Thus the third year is left free for the more difficult poetry of Greek tragedy, in the plays of Aeschylus, Sophocles, and Euripides, with alternative reading in history, oratory, and comedy.

The early accessibility of such great authors in both Latin and Greek and pride in such rapid achievement serve to motivate the students in these accelerated programs and justify the constant demand that they do more than they thought they could. This is the nub of an exciting program in classical languages for the talented: swift progress through a quantity of interesting material, not adjusting to the least able members of the group. Before any such program can be successful, though, there must be present the three elements mentioned in connection with Aristotle, Alexander, and logs: able teachers well trained in the field and conscientious about both their daily and long-term preparation, students who have proven linguistic ability, and classes of comparatively small size sectioned according to ability.

# V

*". . . determined charity"*

# COUNSELING

Joseph E. Fellows
Jill Nooney

THERE ARE TIMES when good classroom teaching is not enough to ensure student success. Despite good intentions and for no apparent reason a student will sometimes stop working or exert only the least possible effort, never getting involved enough to think deeply about the subject or to contribute to the class. Since the others in the class keep up with the assignments and remain interested, the teacher continues to cover the material at the same pace, and the troubled student gets farther and farther behind.

Faced with such puzzling behavior teachers sometimes issue stern words of warning, discipline the student or, more often, offer friendly help and advice. It may turn out that the student is troubled by extreme shyness and finds the Harkness table frightening or is illicitly drinking or finds organizing study time difficult. The student who is shy or lonely might be encouraged to join a club or might be invited to the teacher's apartment for dinner. One who is drinking is told of the dangers and warned of the possibility of being required to leave school. The teacher tells a student who studies compulsively to take an evening off, or helps one who is wasting time to fill out a time chart. These are reasonable responses; they are often met by gratitude and appreciation; many times they work. But when they fail, students may turn to a counselor.

Students seek this kind of help because they cannot explain or cope with—let alone control—the way they feel and act. This lack of understanding and control is because certain important emotional experiences from which the student's difficulties in part spring have been "forgotten"—are not available for recall. The student has come to feel that certain thoughts and feelings are too dangerous to express—dangerous for many reasons.

Imagine a five-year-old boy when his parents bring his newborn sister back from the hospital. When, as frequently happens, the older sibling becomes jealous and angry, the parents usually tolerate this response, and the child gradually adjusts to the new family member. Sometimes, however, for a variety of reasons, the parents find such feelings unacceptable and show their irritation or anger. Sensing this and fearing punishment or loss of love, the older child learns to camouflage, conceal or "forget" these feelings of anger and jealousy. Although such feelings are a natural response to the new situation of having to share his parents with his new sibling, the five-year-old begins to regard the feelings as bad or dangerous.

Repeated often enough such a pattern can leave the individual with the feeling that situations that make him angry must be avoided with singleminded determination. As a student at school, such a boy might find himself doing anything possible to avoid confrontation that might lead to anger. He may, for example, do unreasonable favors for people he hardly even knows, or not even like. He may attempt to read every book on an excessively long reading list or find himself doing anything he can in order to avoid participating in a classroom debate.

The goal of psychotherapy is to reacquaint the student with the forgotten feelings and memories that have blocked his growth in certain areas. By listening actively and empathically the counselor creates an atmosphere of trust that enables the student to talk freely. With the guidance of the counselor the student begins to examine troublesome aspects of his behavior, using childhood memories, recent experiences, and patterns of responses between himself and the counselor as raw material.

Gradually the student develops a growing sense of freedom that allows him to experiment with new ways of responding to old emotionally laden situations. The student who has difficulty expressing anger may try to express how he really feels when the counselor arrives fifteen minutes late for their session. He may refuse to lend his roommate any more money until his outstanding debt has been paid. He may even assert his own opinion in class when he knows it differs from his teacher's. In time the student finds that he is able to cope with difficult situations far better than before.

Consider the story of Jamie, a girl suffering from a problem typical of those experienced by students who seek psychological help. Jamie was an eleventh grader who had been at Exeter for two years. Early in her first year Jamie began finding it difficult to meet deadlines. Even in her second year papers were, with few exceptions, handed in late; her news articles were dashed over to the school newspaper office the morning the paper went to press. She frequently slept through her alarm in the morning, missing study time or her first class. During the first semester of the second year she appeared frequently at the infirmary either requesting sports excuses or complaining of headaches and severe stomach pains. Her medical chart is full of entries that read: "sent upstairs to lie down." Somehow despite the disorganization of her life she managed to maintain honors level grades as well as fulfill all her newspaper obligations. The price she paid was the lack of any feeling of self-worth, pride or any sense of inner peace.

The description of this life of chaos and anxiety was in marked contrast to the appearance of the young woman. She was always neatly and tastefully dressed, hair shining, face scrubbed, and she spoke clearly and animatedly of her internal experiences. In fact if one did not listen to what she was saying, she would have seemed like an unusually mature young person.

Her adviser noticed this paradox and wanted to help her. Since he hoped that a study schedule might serve to organize her life, he got her to agree to meet informally with him twice a week at which time she was to report on her progress. In the beginning Jamie would appear for their meeting contrite and apologetic. She just could not seem to keep to the schedule, even though she thought it might have helped. Sometimes she would sleep through their allotted time, having been up all night dashing off an overdue assignment. Eventually, she began to miss the appointments without explanation and tried to avoid running into him as she did with so many of her teachers for whom she had exhausted her explanations. At this point her adviser became increasingly concerned and suggested that Jamie make an appointment with one of the counselors.

The two met for six months. During the first months Jamie spent much of the time elaborating the ways in which she felt trapped and hopeless. Repeatedly she said: "I feel as if I am about to be crushed by a big boulder I can barely keep ahead of. I have been like this so long. I wake up worried and I go to sleep worried and nothing gets done. It is never going to get better."

A word about her family: Jamie was an only child, who felt that her parents were deeply caring and principled people. In the past ten years they had both become increasingly successful in their careers. Her mother was a professor of pediatric intensive care nursing at a local medical school. Her father was the financial director of a large social service agency, who had written several books, the most recent on fundraising, and frequently traveled to lecture and attend conferences. Jamie considered her mother extremely competent and self-sufficient. She saw her father as a formal, intelligent man, who made a good impression, but was a little soft and basically unsure of himself. In Jamie's eyes he made excessive demands for her mother's attention, requesting constant reassurance and comfort. More than once the mother had shared with Jamie her exasperation at having such a finicky, easily upset husband. On balance Jamie seemed to love and feel proud of her parents, but she was concerned because neither parent could understand why after all those years Jamie, such a capable person, could not seem to pull herself together.

During the sessions Jamie recounted painful experiences. Since she loved to write, she had often thought about the bangup job she could do in her English class writing her autobiography, and when the assignment was given, she looked forward to completing it. As the date approached other assignments also were due. Night followed day with three or four hours of sleep as the first extension and then the second rolled by. Finally her roommate had to type the paper. Over and over this would happen. She related another typical incident that had taken place during Christmas vacation. One afternoon she was experiencing such severe stomach pains that she called a neighbor who took her to the emergency room of the local hospital. After various tests, her mother, who happened to teach at this hospital, brought her home with a clean bill of health. Jamie recalled how sad, lonely and hopeless she felt on returning home. "I felt as though my body and my soul throbbed with ache, and there was just no cure for it."

In the first few months of therapy Jamie called frequently at night, teary, feeling overwhelmed by her inability to cope. On a few occasions she asked for additional appointments on weekends. When visits to the infirmary continued, the counselor began to see her there and one day suggested that perhaps she found something safe and comforting about the infirmary. She agreed with and began to amplify this hypothesis: "It's the only place where I don't feel sick to my stomach. I can actually concentrate here and am able to sleep without waking up in a sweat." The next few sessions were devoted to this theme. The couselor wondered out loud if she felt that the only way she could have someone care for her was by being sick. Perhaps she felt that the only way to attract the attention of her mother, who was so skilled in taking care of the critically ill, was to become ill herself. Once again, she agreed. Maybe, she mused, it was a liability to be healthy and competent.

Several additional sessions were spent talking about this possibility, and gradually Jamie was able to explore her feelings of helplessness. Did this behavior gain her the caring and attention she so badly wanted from her mother? Why was it so hard to ask directly for help? She described again the way in which her father's childish ploys for her mother's attention had met with her mother's criticism. "I feel as though my mother has nothing left for me. She works so hard at the hospital and then has to put up with my father at home. I hate going home." The counselor began to suspect that Jamie's late night calls and requests for extra appointments were tests to see whether her counselor would collapse under the strain of her neediness as she feared her mother would.

Gradually over the months, as trust grew, the number of panicky calls diminished, and her stays in the infirmary tapered off. She began to talk tentatively about her aspirations; she thought about publishing a book of poems at her uncle's printing press in the summer and starting a poetry club the next year. Her articles in the newspaper were zippy and well organized; and her religion teacher mentioned one day how imaginative Jamie's paper on Hermann Hesse had been.

But all the while she continued to present her life outside the office as generally a mess. One morning after Jamie described what a wreck her room was and how angry a teacher had been at her for handing in a paper she hadn't proofread, the counselor asked her about her unwillingness to admit that she was getting better. Did she, like other students, have the feeling that if she got better, she would no longer be able to come and talk. She replied that she did have some of those feelings, and that she also felt guilty about taking up time because other students felt much worse than she did.

By the end of the year we had made considerable progress. Jamie understood that she need not be bleeding to death to be loved or cared for. She was beginning to lead a life somewhat less chaotic than six months before even though she had a way to go before she fully achieved a sense of self-respect and inner serenity.

The story of Jamie shows what professional counseling can do. Like many students Jamie was capable and highly motivated but for hidden reasons felt so miserable that she could not organize her life and could not do as well in class as she would like. Through counseling she was able to take important steps toward understanding herself. For Jamie and students like her, counselors offer a special form of help that others may not be able to provide.

# PHYSICAL EDUCATION

Kathy N. Nekton

JOHN PHILLIPS MAY have had physical education in mind when he urged his instructors in 1781 not only "to enlarge the minds" of their students but also to "regulate" their "tempers" and "encourage" them "to perform some manual labor, such as gardening or the like." Phillips understood how important it is to provide physical education to balance an academic program. Although a large percentage of the students at Exeter and similar schools are intellectually talented, the students of these schools represent only a normal cross section of adolescent physical aptitude. There are splendid athletes; there are also some who are physically inept. Motivation to do well in athletics and interest in physical activity range broadly across a normal spectrum. Such diversity demands a varied program that will stimulate and meet the needs of all the students.

In a demanding academic environment, it is important to encourage the growth and development of the whole person, for if students are to function academically, they must maintain healthy bodies. More than that, physical education is a basic part of education both at school and in later life. The body provides each individual with a medium for learning and expression; physical education can help each person learn to use his body—how to move. Movement is learning. Consider the infant, who begins life, not with words, but with bending and stretching. Wallace Stevens describes this part of education:

> A moving part of motion...
> A changing part of change,
> ...a discovery...
> Part of a discovery...
> Too much like thinking
> to be less than thought.[1]

Ideally, students will develop a joy in movement that will be sustained for a lifetime.

Schools can help students find this joy in a variety of ways. For students who want to be a part of a team, but lack the ability or the time to commit themselves to a varsity sport there are intramural athletics. If the school is large enough, players can be divided according to age, size, and ability so that students will have a good chance to find their proper level of involvement, intensity and ability. For instance, the school can offer one level of ice hockey for beginning and intermediate skaters and another for experienced competitors. This opportunity to compete at the proper level is precious because it ordinarily vanishes once students leave school.

But the intramural system has little relevance for those who are indifferent to competition—or even to physical activity in general. It is often possible to pique the interest of these students by offering instructional classes in a wide selection of recreational sports that carry over for a lifetime. Enjoyable activities such as golf, tennis and bicycling can provide the motivation to exercise because they do not bear the connotations that the sedentary soul has associated with "gym class." Since many such students lack interest in any sort of physical movement at all, instructional classes are often the most difficult to teach. But there are ways to get the reluctant interested. In bicycling, for example, the instructor can sometimes lure an unsuspecting student by bringing out a map and asking the cyclist to plan the trip for the class. Good academic students, furthermore, possess such an intense desire to learn that if they are challenged properly they will do their part, and learning will take place. Teachers can derive satisfaction from kindling interest in these students and from knowing that this interest will help them live longer, healthier lives.

There are also the needs of the youngest students. The one hundred or so boys and girls who enter the ninth grade at Exeter each fall span the scale physically, mentally, and emotionally, representing the smallest but the most diverse group of the four classes. In athletics they are on the bottom rung of the ladder, kept there by the older students. The situation calls for a special learning experience.

We have tried to provide this experience with a special program for ninth graders during the fall and winter sports seasons. The program meets four mornings a week with the following individual daily schedule:

Fall Program
10:25—10:50 a.m. Fitness Training
10:55—11:20 a.m. Sports skill #1
11:25—11:50 a.m. Sports skill #2

Winter Program
10:25—11:05 a.m. Sports skill #1
11:10—11:50 a.m. Sports skill #2

The first goal of the program is to improve individual body fitness. A battery of tests administered at the start of the program and at the end gives all students a point of comparison with national norms and also offers them a chance to see how much they have improved in six months. After the tests are taken in September all students seek to improve their fitness by spending the first half hour each morning exercising in one of four fitness training areas: weight training, cross-country running, an obstacle course, and basic calisthenics.

The second goal of the program is to expose the students to as many athletic opportunities as possible. By the end of the winter the ninth graders have tried virtually every sport offered at Exeter by taking minicourses in small groups of about twelve taught by professional physical educators who specialize in the particular activity. In this setting, enthusiasm spreads easily, involving students in sports they never experienced before. It is not unusual to see boys trying field hockey or girls learning flag football.

Perhaps most satisfying of all is the third goal of the program: to construct an environment that promotes class unity, personal identity and a feeling of self-worth. Since the program is small and limited to ninth graders, the members of the class soon get to know each other. Because the students are placed according to ability levels, they learn at approximately the same rate and are not constantly outdistanced by better athletes. In the team competition that ends the program the students choose the sports in which they wish to compete. As a result they are able to contribute to their teams where they feel strongest or in the areas they enjoy most. The beginning squash player has the chance to push his team into first place by winning a match at his own level. Students can develop a sense of self-worth by acting as leaders of activities. A weak student can feel proud at the end of the survival swimming class by managing to stay afloat for thirty minutes with hands and feet tied.

The last extension of physical activity is the interscholastic program, which attracts the students most vitally interested, most talented, and most highly motivated. In a school for the academically gifted, the coaches of interscholastic athletic teams face special problems. First is the challenge of trying to accomplish a great deal in a short space of time, for the school day involves time commitments to many areas, all of which demand the most out of the student. Such demands take their toll, leaving even athletes who love their sports tired and unable to generate enthusiasm. Coaches must then become magicians, actors, teachers and guidance counselors disguised in warm-up jackets, approaching each day with a multiple purpose. Training the athlete's body to perform the intricate maneuvers needed in the sport is hard enough; directing the athlete's mind and integrating it with the body is where the real teaching occurs. The products of the classroom—often tired of being challenged, tired of competing and feeling mediocre among students who excel—are sometimes so emotionally drained that they have trouble pushing themselves to hard physical training. Tired or not, varsity athletes are sometimes preoccupied with the moment and little interested in ultimate goals.

These are not easy problems to solve. Each coach approaches them differently. One method that has met with great success is to return to old-fashioned team spirit. The coach allows, indeed encourages, the athletes to express youthful enthusiasm by cheering, putting up posters and wearing team shirts. It also helps if the coach also joins in the fun. Once generated, this uninhibited behavior develops into pride for the team, and responsibility to the team becomes a personal commitment.

Another method is for the coach to spend time with each athlete individually, establishing rapport and reinforcing the athlete's self-confidence. Coaches should evaluate and reevaluate their players' ability and their standing in competition. Coaches can also assign extra work for certain players to do outside of regular practice in order to help them develop skills such as cradling in lacrosse or serving in tennis. The point is to give the athlete individual attention.

The root of any successful program is strong leadership. Because many schools believe in involving all their faculty in every phase of school life, those who teach academic subjects at these schools must also coach. This double role gives the teacher greater contact with the students and improves rapport. While some faculty members come to the program with a wealth of experience, knowledge and enthusiasm, others have enthusiasm, but little firsthand knowledge of the sport in which they are involved. Because the athletic expertise of faculty members varies, the role of the professional physical educator takes on a special significance. Having spent four to eight years studying all phases of physical education from volleyball to advanced physiology and biomechanics, the professionals are able to provide indispensable teaching and leadership. They are able to train faculty members by giving daily lesson plans and offering new ideas and methods.

Physical educators should strive to maintain solid backgrounds by constantly bringing their skills up-to-date. This specialization gives the coaches deeper understanding of sports and makes them better qualified to share personal skills and knowledge with the students. That which is most people's Saturday afternoon entertainment is a coach's business. The physical educator's classrooms are the pools, courts and playing fields. It is not unusual for a hockey coach to attend dozens of games a season played by other teams. Each game is a study, like a new book read, providing answers and new ideas. Professional journals report the latest research in new fields such as sports medicine and sports psychology. Since the national governing bodies of each sport set the tone for the programs nationwide, involvement in these keeps the professional informed. Perhaps most crucial is an awareness of what is occurring in collegiate sports because secondary schools prepare students to enter institutions of higher learning. Whether varsity athletes or recreational tennis players, high school graduates should possess the skills to fit into their new environments. The coach can be a vital link and a personal contact for students making college plans.

Teaching ability is further enhanced when the teacher is involved physically as well as intellectually. Although it is not imperative for coaches to participate directly in the sports in which they instruct, they achieve a higher level of credibility if they do. Students appreciate seeing an adult training at the same level at which they are asked to train. In addition, the adult gains useful knowledge from this active experience. Having endured the same physical stress as the athletes, a forty-year-old may realize that fifteen-year-olds can, in fact should, be asked to do more—or maybe less—than they are presently doing. Or coaches may gain greater insights into mental trouble spots in their training regimens after having experienced them firsthand. If coaches also participate in formal competition, insight deepens. Presently Exeter, for example, has coaches competing in masters' track (a seventy-year-old emeritus), masters' swimming, statewide tennis, squash, marathon and road races, horse shows and golf. We can all serve as role models for our students, combining intellectual curiosity in professional and nonprofessional areas.

Physical educators must be more than simply technicians passing on the fundamentals of their subject matter. They must, of course, provide the athlete with technical skills, but they must also educate the whole person. It is exciting to think how much can be done to help athletes learn in this broader sense—and frightening to know how much can be left undone. Athletics—especially games—provide an excellent medium for learning and for passing on time-honored values. Team sports can generate skills in working cooperatively—each individual part of the whole. The coach, for example, has the opportunity to remove from a game a player who is not doing his part in the overall team plan. Unlike the situation in the real world, the player has the chance to discuss the reasons for his removal and then to go back into the game with a better understanding of his role. The coach can also teach the team how to support the weaker members, for everyone soon realizes that opponents always key on the weakest player. If the weaker players are not given this support by their stronger teammates, internal conflicts develop and the team suffers. Individual players—strong and weak alike—must learn to play in such a way that the whole unit benefits.

Not all learning is designed to promote the group over the individual. Real teaching also occurs when the teacher can get the athlete to begin developing a perceptive, self-analytical mind. The athlete and the coach become partners as the athlete seeks heightened kinesthetic awareness. Videotapes and a small student-teacher ratio can help the coach take a student from simple to complex tasks. And once learned, each skill forms the basis for additional learning. During the process the teacher can ask the student questions such as, "How did that feel?" "What was your arm doing?" "Tell me what was wrong with that?" The ability to begin to answer these questions indicates that the athlete has joined in the educational process.

Students find out a great deal about themselves emotionally while on the courts, rinks or in the pool because the combined physical and mental stress of athletics provides a special learning situation. While competing on a team, athletes may decide that the conformity to a group and proximity to others that a team demands are not appealing. They may decide that an individual sport provides a different, more compatible set of challenges. They discover how much self-discipline they possess and what their ability is to reach beyond what they feel are their limitations. To help this learning process, coaches design practice sessions on a progressive basis, building one skill upon another. When they believe that the athlete's physical skills are sufficiently developed for safety, coaches test the athlete mentally as well as physically. The test may be a thirty-minute survival session in the water, a back handspring on the balance beam for the first time, or a five-mile run after a long practice. Whatever the sport the test is a necessary experience for personal growth. Sometimes the process of training and the ability to overcome pain and fear become more important than the skill performed.

The teacher-coach guides the student-athlete in the learning-training process. Individuals are important, and in order for each to feel successful a variety of goals are drawn up, each proportional to a person's skills and abilities. It is vital for individuals to enjoy what they are doing by developing self-esteem through successful participation. Ultimately the goal is to develop well-balanced educated persons, who see and experience the overlap in all areas of learning. The student-athletes apply their mathematics and physics in the laws of body mechanics to understand the difference between power and speed. The knowledge of physical movement enables them to appreciate movement in art as caught by the great sculptors and painters. They follow the progress of sport with an historical eye from the Greek marathoners to modern Olympians. They learn to cooperate and communicate in order to help form a team. Most important, they learn the joy of movement, the freedom of expression on a nonverbal level, the rhythm and music of motion—in Wallace Stevens' words "a discovery...like thinking."

1. Wallace Stevens, "Looking Across the Fields and Watching the Birds Fly," quoted in Eleanor Metheny, *Movement and Meaning*, (New York, McGraw-Hill Book Co., 1968), p. 92.

# MORAL EDUCATION

Charles L. Terry

*But above all, it is expected that the attention of instructors to the disposition of the minds and morals of the youth under their charge will exceed every other care; well considering that though goodness without knowledge is weak and feeble, yet knowledge without goodness is dangerous, and that both united form the noblest character; and lay the surest foundation of usefulness to mankind.*

> John Phillips in the
> *Original Deed of Gift,*
> Phillips Exeter Academy,
> *1781*

As JOHN PHILLIPS perceptively noted, teachers must be concerned with moral education as well as with the dispensation of knowledge. His admonition is imperative today for those charged with the education of adolescents; but few will agree on how best to combine goodness and knowledge. Lawrence Kohlberg, the most prominent thinker in this country on moral education, for the most part agrees with the Platonic assumption that goodness is the result of the compelling knowledge of principled conduct. And teachers, some at Exeter, by and large seem to assume that questions of goodness are to be answered exclusively in the terms of knowledge.

John Phillips, on the other hand, was not a Platonist, for he did not assume that knowledge, even knowledge of goodness, compelled men to be moral. He was wise enough to discern that intellectual distinction can breed selfishness and cynicism; unaccompanied by a spirit of charity, unaccompanied by a dedication to service, knowledge can be "dangerous." Were he here today, he would aver that the Platonic formula is blind to the frequent disparity between judgment and action.

Most secondary schools do much better in knowledge than in goodness—particularly those engaged in the uncompromising pursuit of academic excellence. Instead of the link between knowledge and goodness that Phillips envisioned, there is more likely to be, at best, a potentially creative tension between them. For a teacher of gifted students in a boarding school the experience of the classroom and the experience of the dormitory can be radically different ones; and often the fulfillment of the classroom can be a bewildering contrast to the frustration of the dormitory. It is possible, for example, to read an eloquent student essay on King Lear's discovery of charity and to see that same student act uncharitably toward other students in the dormitory.

The problem is, to a great extent, that students are inclined to see a sharp division between what they call "academics" on the one hand and social development on the other. They are willing, nay eager, to grant a teacher authority in the classroom, but they often fiercely challenge that teacher's authority in their residential life. And even in the classroom they are not always willing to accept the teacher's authority in terms of values, except for the value of rigorous critical analysis. They recognize a teacher's authority in furnishing them with a method, a method, significantly, that enables them to experiment with ideas, and even in some academic disciplines to see ambiguity not only as tolerable, but perhaps desirable. Given this point of view, it is logical for them to expect that if our institutions are consistent, we will provide the same kind of opportunity for flexibility in the residential life of the school that we provide in the classroom.

In a way they are implicitly stating what people who have spent much time and thought on moral education have recently concluded. For a number of years Lawrence Kohlberg has favored a didactic scheme for moral education, based on classroom discussions of moral dilemmas. But recently he and others have been moving toward a contextual scheme — specifically the creation of a "just community" in schools, a "just community" because students themselves are given a major role in the governance of such a community.

But what if the faculty in a boarding school determines that such a democratic process is not sound education and that it is an inordinately time-consuming process? In that case a kind of full-fledged contextual education is not viable. Furthermore, what if students are reluctant to accept the responsibility for enforcing such rules or agreements as they themselves have had a significant role in establishing? In boarding schools these conditions frequently obtain, so that in fairness to their students and, moreover, in fairness to the parents of those students, faculties are wary of following Kohlberg's model of a "just community."

But faculties have been equally wary of what they often consider faddish classroom discussions and the exhortations of the didactic approach. We are in troubled waters for we are skeptical of both didactic moral education and of contextual moral education, which entitles students to have a major role in the governance of their community. Perhaps it is possible, nevertheless, to blend the didactic and the contextual approaches in a way that will take advantage of the culture of our school.

What we need to look at are the implicit values of our community—the "hidden curriculum," if you will. These implicit values usually create what two of our colleagues, who were also participants in our Summer Institute on Moral Education in 1978, have called "sophisticated selfishness." In "The Residential School as a Moral Environment," Harvard Knowles and David Weber offer this analysis:

> . . . all of us have known students who graduated from our schools with highly distinguished academic records but with minimal interest in other people, with imperceptible commitments to compassion or service. But most or all of us want to work in schools that try to nourish and that *tend* to nourish a less selfish orientation toward life; we want to create environments which encourage generosity of spirit and principled decision-making, not sophisticated selfishness, in our students and ourselves.[1]

In order to create such an environment we need to ask ourselves questions about the ethos of our institutions. The earnest and genuine rhetoric of our catalog statements aside, what do we really stand for? What values are embedded in the quality of our living? How in our daily routine do we communicate moral principles to each other—faculty to faculty;

1. *The Phillips Exeter Academy Bulletin*, Vol. LXXVIII (November 1978), p. 15.

students to students; and each group to the other? We have always been moral educators whether we intended to be or not; we need to make ourselves intentional moral educators—in both the didactic and contextual modes—and to help those of our colleagues reluctant to assume the role to become intentional moral educators.

What are our goals as such intentional moral educators? Knowles and Weber argue that "determined charity" should be at the center of our life as a community; "determined charity" is the antithesis of and the antidote to "sophisticated selfishness." Largely as a result of the atmosphere of ruthless academic competition in schools most likely to attract gifted students, "sophisticated selfishness" seems to the gifted, no matter how perceptive in other respects, the school's unofficial badge of attendance and even of graduation. How do we convince them that appearances to the contrary, this is not what our pride in academic achievement is supposed to produce?

Let us go back to the student who writes eloquently on King Lear's discovery of charity, but who leaves the classroom and returns to the dormitory demonstrating in his treatment of other students a distinct absence of charity. To this student such inconsistency is, as we have already remarked, defensible. However, it is also possible to see this student act uncharitably toward his classmates in the very class in which he wrote the essay. We might argue, then, that the first way to "form the minds and morals of the youth," in Phillips' phrase, is to enable them to see the reasonableness of transferring intellectual convictions to social ones in the classroom. Indeed, such transferring of learning to life can be the most exciting experience available to the young; and what more promising way to bring about a commerce of intellectual and social activity than that available in such a classroom atmosphere as in Exeter's Harkness system—a dozen students sitting around a table with their teacher, the students with guidance from the teacher, assuming the burden of the discussion. The system offers the ideal setting for a subtle combination of contextual and didactic moral education.

In such a context the students can begin to see that the success of the class depends as much, maybe even more, on its social chemistry, on its spirit of tolerance and openness, as it does on the ability of its members to think rapidly and to be highly verbal. If the teacher accedes to the radical wisdom in the statement "the 'subject matter' of the lesson [is] the responses of the learners to the questions they confront," then perhaps the students can begin to incorporate this attitude into their conviction of what is most fundamental in the process of learning.[2] Teachers and students may begin to treat each other with the "determined charity" that Knowles and Weber call for.

In becoming intentional moral educators, teachers and students have the rare opportunity of striving toward being a model of what an educated human being realizes: "the noblest character," to borrow Phillips' phrase, is one in which mind and heart are perfectly integrated, poised in a balance. In a recent book, *Promoting Moral Growth: From Piaget to Kohlberg*, the authors note that "moral judgment is the area in which Piaget has dealt most explicitly with the relationship between cognition and affect"; and they go on to offer this definition: "For what is moral judgment if not a cognitive structuring of how we feel we ought to treat others and how others ought to treat us?"[3] It is this kind of passionate intelligence that students can encounter in the final awareness of Gabriel Conroy, the principal character in Joyce's greatest story, *The Dead*. Conroy, an example of moral growth in fiction if ever there was one, thinks deeply because he feels deeply and vice versa. If such an experience is at the heart of moral education, then perhaps moral education is really what schools are most fundamentally about.

Even though gifted students are usually intent upon being independent of the teacher's values, it is possible to confront them with powerful moral ideas that form the thematic core of a course or part of it. Students can be made aware of the critical moral issues imbedded in what would otherwise be a routine set of assignments. In a course in chemistry, for example, the teacher can turn a unit on chemical reactions or acid or combustion into moral education by focusing attention on burning coal (carbon) and such impurities as sulphur. Students can be asked to discuss what goes up the smokestack besides carbon dioxide,

2. Neil Postman and Charles Weingartner, *Teaching As a Subversive Activity*, (New York, Delacorte Press, 1969), p. 75.

3. Richard H. Hersh, Diana P. Paolitto and Joseph Reimer, *Promoting Moral Growth: From Piaget to Kohlberg* (New York, Longman, 1979), p. 39.

water and soot. As soon as they learn that sulphur dioxide dissolves to form a weak acid, they can quite naturally engage in a discussion of acid rain. Then the discussion can move along to the question of whether pollution control should be local or regional, where the jurisdictions no longer coincide with those that provide the political or legal power. By this time the class is discussing the broader issue of what to do when problems transcend our controlling social structures. The students are deeply involved as they begin to take a stand on conflicting answers to technical, social and ultimately moral questions.

It is difficult to teach American History without engaging in moral issues. In dealing with the middle of the 19th century from the election of Andrew Jackson in 1828 to the end of Reconstruction in 1877 there is no better theme than the effect of racial attitudes on public and private policy. Instead of concentrating on the political conflicts between Jackson and John C. Calhoun and between Abraham Lincoln and Stephen A. Douglas, it can be more rewarding to ask students to consider the underlying influence of racial attitudes on these men and their actions. How do the students explain the paradox of Jackson's belief in democracy and his defense of slavery? Between Calhoun's insistence on liberty and his conviction that slavery should be the basis of Southern society? Ask students to decide whether they would have gone to war to destroy or defend the institution of slavery. Ask students to look at the issue of human rights through the eyes of Frederick Douglass or Jefferson Davis. And in dealing with Reconstruction ask the members of the class to decide how they would have dealt with the freedmen after the Civil War. Would they have cared more about human rights or sectional peace? The parallel between the moral issues in the 1860s and those in the 1960s will readily become apparent.[4]

An entire English course can be shaped around a moral issue. At Exeter, for example, one teacher has built a semester course for seniors around the theme of charity in *King Lear*, *Paradise Lost* and *The Brothers Karamazov*. At the start the students have been given Knowles and Weber's article on moral education as their first assignment. It is a useful assignment because

4. I am grateful to Donald B. Cole for this paragraph on teaching American history and to C. Arthur Compton for the preceding paragraph on teaching chemistry.

the conclusions in the article are inductively based on instances of school life that are a part of the student's immediate experience. The assignment is also pedagogically sound because students get to become critics of two teachers' writing, and this offers a special kind of engagement for them: they see dedicated people trying to come to grips with the meaning of their professional work. Given the subject, "The Residential School as a Moral Environment," they also see those teachers' intense personal involvement in their profession.

It may be outrageously tendentious to open a course declaring that "determined charity" should be a major goal of the class for itself, and by extension for those students' larger involvement in the community, but when they realize that three works as diverse as *King Lear*, *Paradise Lost* and *The Brothers Karamazov* are vitally linked by the theme of love they get a glimpse of how great writers give "a cognitive structuring of how we feel we ought to treat others and how others ought to treat us." Lear's awareness of the inhumanity of rational attitudes toward existence which deny love and human responsibility for our fellow man is as indelible as Alyosha Karamazov's awareness of the truth of Father Zossima's dictum: "Hell is the inability to love." The brilliant tyrant of Hell, Milton's Satan, a notorious example of "sophisticated selfishness," is for students reduced to eating ashes as the real drama of the poem becomes the simple heroism of two fallen human beings reconciling themselves to each other in unselfish love.

Gifted students must ultimately be purged of the cant that "academics" are mere methodology, or that "facts," as they sometimes disdainfully say, have nothing to do with one's social and emotional being. The classroom *is* the center of our schools, and we should affirm that idea boldly, at the same time redressing the balance in those classrooms so that intellect and emotion are as perfectly integrated as we can make them. And then, superb day, our classrooms will be the models for the larger community, and we will know when we pursue "excellence" just what we mean by that word.

# THE AUTHORS

RICHARD G. BROWN has taught mathematics at Exeter since 1964 except for a year as visiting lecturer at the University of Arizona. He has published a series of textbooks including *Basic Geometry* and *Advanced Mathematics, An Introductory Course.*

DAVID D. COFFIN taught classics at Smith College before joining the Department of Classical Languages at Exeter in 1953. He has served as chairman of the Latin Advanced Placement Committee and has been assistant chief reader for the Latin Advanced Placement examination. He is co-author of *A Teacher's Notebook: Latin* and *Beginning an Advanced Placement Classics Course.*

DONALD B. COLE has been teaching history at Exeter since 1947. He has read Advanced Placement examinations in American History and has served as chairman of the Committee on Teaching of the American Historical Association. Among his publications are *The Preparation of Secondary School History Teachers.*

C. ARTHUR COMPTON came to Exeter in 1955 after three years at Mount Hermon School. At Exeter he has taught both physics and chemistry. He has contributed to *The Physics Teacher, American Journal of Physics, School Science and Mathematics,* and *The Journal of Chemical Education.* He also participated in the Harvard Project Physics.

ROBERT H. CORNELL was a mathematics instructor at Berwick Academy in Maine and at Lincoln-Sudbury and Concord high schools in Massachusetts before coming to Exeter in 1966. At Exeter he teaches mathematics, physics, and photography.

MARY T. DEVAULT came to Exeter in 1978 after having been a teacher of theology in Westchester, N.Y., and the Principal of Dominican High School in Detroit. She is currently Acting Chairman of the Department of Religion.

JOSEPH E. FELLOWS served in the Peace Corps in Nepal, taught mathematics at Northfield-Mount Hermon School, and directed the Guidance Department at Holliston High School in Massachusetts. Since 1976 he has been a Counselor at Exeter.

A. IRVING FORBES taught music in Colebrook and Portsmouth, N.H., and in Kittery, Maine, before coming to Exeter in 1959, where he is Chairman of the Department of Music. He has been principal bassoonist with the Portland (Maine) Symphony Orchestra and conductor of the Rockingham Choral Society.

E. Arthur Gilcreast is presently Chairman of the Department of History, Instructor in Business, and varsity crew coach at Exeter, where he began teaching in 1967. He has been a reader for the Advanced Placement examinations in American history.

Janet E. Kehl has taught at St. Stephen's School in Rome as well as at Exeter, where she has been teaching French since 1970. Her M.A.T. degree at Yale is in both English and French.

David B. McIlhiney was the Episcopal chaplain at Dartmouth College. He has published articles on religious education, and was Instructor of Anthropology and Religion at St. Andrew's College in Laurinburg, N.C. He has taught religion at Exeter since 1977 and is currently School Minister.

Kathy N. Nekton has coached field hockey, swimming, and lacrosse at Exeter since 1973. She is currently Acting Chairman of the Department of Physical Education and a member of the New England Masters Swim Club.

Jill Nooney was formerly a Psychiatric Social Worker at the Dartmouth-Hitchcock Mental Health Center. She has been a Counselor at Exeter since 1978.

Norval W. Rindfleisch has taught English, first at Pomfret and, since 1968, at Exeter. He has graded Advanced Placement examinations in English, has served as teacher consultant for the Bay Area Writing Project at the University of California, and has been assistant director of the Exeter Writing Project. He has published stories in the *Yale Literary Magazine* and the *Literary Review*. His latest publication is *The Dissertation and the Partnership*.

Donald P. Schultz taught theater and history at Ann Arbor High School before coming to Exeter in 1966. He now serves as Chairman of the Department of Drama, Director of the Fisher Theater, and an Instructor in History.

Charles L. Terry has taught English at Dartmouth College and, since 1967, at Exeter. He was the Director of the Summer Institute on Moral Education held at Exeter in 1978 and is the editor of *Knowledge Without Goodness Is Dangerous: Moral Education in Boarding Schools*.

ALSO PUBLISHED BY
The Phillips Exeter Academy Press

*Knowledge Without Goodness Is Dangerous: Moral Education in Boarding Schools*. Charles L. Terry, Editor. 1981